Salad Days

HOME COOKING

Salad Days

BY

THE EDITORS OF TIME-LIFE BOOKS

TIME-LIFE/GEDDES & GROSSET

Contents

Salad's Special Magic

What fresher, more inviting food is there than salad? It seems to radiate good health, and so it should: the tenderest of greens, the crunchiest of roots, the leanest of meats and poultry, the most nutritious seafood, the most wholesome of grains, beans and pasta are among its raw materials. And, as if this in itself were not advertisement enough of salad's virtues, it is a dish than need not be fussed over, and one that can often be made quickly.

A salad can be the most varied of dishes. It may be as simple as a bowl of lettuce tossed with a light vinaigrette, or a more complex composition of meats and vegetables that might serve as a meal. Its elements can be either raw or cooked, or a

mixture of the two, and it can be served chilled, at room temperature, or even warm.

Even the ancient Greeks knew that salad was healthy; they held it to be a food of the gods. In Shakespearean England, so-called fountains of youth, assembled from the first tender herbs and lettuces of spring, were eagerly consumed as antidotes to the grim winter diet. The great French gastronome Brillat-Savarin summed it up nicely: 'Salad refreshes without weakening and comforts without irritating,' he wrote in 1825, 'and it makes us younger.'

Whether truly rejuvenating or not, salad is, with its endless choice of ingredients, a bountiful source of minerals, vitamins and other nutrients. And when it is dressed carefully, salad will be low in fat as well, and thus in calories. The fact that most types of lettuce are between 90 and 95 per cent water is bound to give some people reason to cheer.

Salads made with grains, dried beans or pasta are loaded with complex carbohydrates—the main source of energy for the human body—and protein. Dried beans offer a particularly generous supply of fibre and protein; but for all their protein to be utilized by the body, they must be coupled with other foods that offer complementary proteins. As luck would have it, many of these are the very ingredients of successful modern salads—wheat, rice, meat and dairy products, to list a few.

As this book makes patently clear, salad need never be the same from one meal to the next. The salad maker today is aided greatly by the presence of once-exotic ingredients in the supermarket, including a wider variety of fresh herbs.

The range of available vinegars and salad oils has increased as well, along with the number of different prepared mustards. Wine, tarragon, balsamic and Chinese black vinegars lend a new liveliness to salad dressings, as do oils as diverse as walnut, almond and dark sesame.

Freshness above all

Our salad bounty is enhanced still further by the seasonal appearance of several delightful ingredients. Asparagus might well stand as the emblem of spring; tomatoes plump and red from basking in the sun evoke summer, as does golden sweetcorn, its kernels swollen with sweet juice. Cabbages and root vegetables show up abundantly in autumn. Many of the recipes in this volume would greatly benefit from the inclusion of vegetables picked at their peak of ripeness and flavour. Faster, improved transport and distribution, as well as local produce stalls in street markets, make this possible by putting an array of perfectly ripened ingredients at the salad-maker's disposal.

Fruit has played a time-honoured role in many salads. A greater availability of seasonal produce and an increase in creativity have left the dieter's staple of yore—a canned peach half topped with a scoop of cottage cheese and served on a bed of tasteless limp lettuce—happily outmoded. New marriages of fruit and meat, seafood and vegetables have taken place.

Although the recipes call for fresh ingredients, salads of course can be a wonderful vehicle for leftovers. Providing they have not been previously buttered, cooked green beans, well chilled from their overnight stay in the refrigerator, make a lively luncheon dish when tossed with a vinaigrette. Likewise, leftover poultry and meats lend themselves to intriguing combinations with greens, fresh herbs and simple dressings.

Simplicity as a goal

With limitless possibilities for salads, the temptation has often been to put in too much. One recipe from the 17th century calls for almonds, raisins, figs, spinach, olives, capers, currants, sage, cucumbers, red cabbage, orange and lemon. Our cooks have been more selective, balancing flavours and bearing in mind a particular salad's place in the meal as first course, main course or side dish. They have mixed complementary greens and paired foods and seasonings that share a natural affinity, such as tomatoes and basil, rice and saffron, cucumber and dill. At the same time, the cooks have sought contrasts in texture, combining, for instance, dried apricots, wild rice and water chestnuts.

The recipes have been designed to encourage imaginative, well-balanced eating. Serving portions are based on whether a salad is to be eaten as a side dish or a starter, as a main course at lunch, or as a main course at dinner. Salads with cooked ingredients are generally served in smaller portions because they are more substantial than raw salads. If you wish to serve larger portions, which means more calories, take into account the rest of the day's eating in your menu planning and compensate for the increased calories by selecting appropriate foods.

The first section of the book explores some unusual combinations of greens, vegetables and fruits. The second delves into grains, dried beans and pasta, while the third serves up salads based on meats, poultry and seafood. In the last section, the microwave oven offers shortcuts to salad-making.

Whatever the components of a salad, it is the dressing that ties them together. In this book, each dressing has been created with an eye to limiting the fat and calories, generally through a reduction in the amount of oil used. Still, even reduced-oil dressing must contain calories. Thus anyone seriously concerned about lowering caloric intake should use a dressing sparingly, pouring on just enough to moisten and flavour the salad.

Handling salad ingredients

The success of a salad—particularly one calling for greens—depends greatly on how the ingredients are handled beforehand. If the salad is to be truly delicious, only the freshest of produce will do. Select greens that are crisp and well coloured. (The darker the lettuces, the more vitamin A they will contain.)

The greens should be washed under cold running water. With head lettuce, pluck away the leaves and pay particular attention to their bases, where soil may cling. Discard any leaves that are wilted, have frayed edges or are blemished. Grit-prone greens—spinach, for example—will come clean when gently swirled several times in a one or more bowls of water. Once they have been washed, the greens should be removed from the water, drained and then carefully dried—either by patting them between paper towels or by whirling them in a salad spinner. The removal of clinging water ensures that the dressing will coat the salad evenly and that the leaves will remain crisp.

If the washed greens are not to be used immediately, they may be stored for a day in the refrigerator, in a plastic bag, with paper towel wrapped around them to soak up any excess moisture. Fresh herbs also benefit from respectful treatment; packed loosely in a closed container, they will remain vigorous a week or more in the refrigerator. Some cooks trim the stems, particularly of herbs that come in bunches, then stand the herbs in a glass or jar filled with water and keep them in the refrigerator lightly covered with plastic film.

For a natural-looking salad, tear the lettuce leaves by hand into pieces of the size you want—unless, of course, the recipe specifies otherwise. To preserve crispness, do this shortly before the salad is to be served and be sure to apply the dressing at the very last minute. Then toss or otherwise mix the salad.

Perhaps the wisest words about salad preparation are some that date back three centuries. 'Every plant should bear its part without being overpowered by some herb of stronger taste, so as to endanger the native savour and virtue of the rest,' wrote English diarist John Evelyn in 1699. When this is accomplished, all the ingredients should 'fall into their places like notes in music'. Thus carefully orchestrated, the salad will win applause as one of the liveliest, most satisfying and healthiest parts of the meal.

The Burgeoning of the Greens

Salad making has benefited immeasurably from the increasing availability of hitherto esoteric or hard-to-find greens. Some of these are shown here and on the next three pages, with accompanying descriptions of their virtues. Among them are two vegetables, kale and beet greens, that take on a new life when eaten raw in salads.

Rocket (arugula). An Italian green, rocket has a pungent, slightly peppery flavour. Look for small, narrow leaves—signal of a young, sweet plant.

Beet greens. Use only the freshest, youngest greens, discarding the red stems. The leaves have a flavour that resembles both spinach and beetroot.

Chicory. Sharp in flavour and crisp in texture, the finest chicory has tightly wrapped leaves that range in colour from white to pale yellow.

Curly endive. This resembles chicory in flavour. Although the lighter leaves are sweeter and more tender than the dark green ones, they still boast the tangy bite that is associated with all endives.

Dandelion greens. Part of the chicory family, dandelion greens should be eaten before the flower appears. Young leaves can be blanched by inverting a flowerpot over the plant.

Batavian endive (escarole). This broad-leaved relative of curly endive shares its cousin's pleasingly bitter flavour. It is best used in combination with sweeter greens.

Kale. A relative newcomer to the salad bowl, kale is an excellent source of vitamin C. Only the youngest leaves should be used, and many cooks prefer to shred them—they can be tough.

Lamb's Lettuce (corn salad, mâche). Chewy but not crisp, this delicate green has a nutlike sweetness, with an underlying astringency. It complements dressings made with nuts and oils.

The Burgeoning of the Greens

Mustard greens (green-in-snow, Chinese mustard). With their pungent flavour, young mustard greens marry well with less assertive salad greens. Avoid the older, tougher leaves.

Chinese cabbage (Chinese leaves). This elongated cabbage has long, broad ribs and crinkled, white to light green leaves. Select unblemished heads with firm leaves.

Oakleaf lettuce. Among the most delicate of lettuces, oakleaf does not travel well. When available, however, it is well worth the purchase.

Radicchio. This purplish red Italian chicory is sought for its chewy texture and slightly bitter taste. Italians call it 'the flower that can be eaten'.

Savoy cabbage. The mildest form of head cabbage, Savoy can be used in salads where the taste of other cabbages would be too strong. Be sure the leaves are crisp.

Sorrel. A leaf vegetable resembling spinach, sorrel tastes of lemon. Use only the youngest leaves. When cooking sorrel, avoid reactive vessels and utentsils; these can turn sorrel black and give a metalic taste.

Watercress. An acquatic green, watercress has a refreshing peppery flavour. But bright green bunches with thin stems. Watercress can be refrigerated with its stems in water to keep it fresh.

The Key to Better Eating

Home Cooking addresses the concerns of today's weight-conscious, health-minded cooks with recipes that take into account guidelines set by nutritionists. The secret of eating well, of course, has to do with maintaining a balance of foods in the diet. The recipes thus should be used thoughtfully, in the context of a day's eating. To make the choice easier, an analysis is given of nutrients in a single serving. The counts for calories, protein, cholesterol, total fat, saturated fat and sodium are approximate.

Interpreting the chart

The chart below gives dietary guidelines for healthy men, women and children. Recommended figures vary from country to country, but the principles are the same everywhere. Here, the average daily amounts of calories and protein are from a report by the UK Department of Health and Social Security; the maximum advisable daily intake of fat is based on guidelines given by the National Advisory Committee on Nutrition Education (NACNE); those for cholesterol and sodium are based on upper limits suggested by the World Health Organization.

The volumes in the Home Cooking series do not purport to be diet books, nor do they focus on health foods. Rather, they express a common-sense approach to cooking that uses salt, sugar, cream, butter and oil in moderation while employing other ingredients that also provide flavour and satisfaction. The portions themselves are modest in size.

The recipes make few unusual demands. Naturally they call for fresh ingredients, offering substitutes when these are unavailable. (The substitute is not calculated in the nutrient analysis, however.) Most of the ingredients can be found in any well-stocked supermarket.

Heavy-bottomed pots and pans are recommended to guard against burning whenever a small amount of oil is used and where there is danger of the food adhering to the hot surface, but non-stick pans can be utilized as well. Both safflower oil and virgin olive oil are favoured for sautéing. Safflower oil was chosen because it is the most highly polyunsaturated vegetable fat available in supermarkets, and polyunsaturated fats reduce blood cholesterol; if unobtainable, use sunflower oil, also high in polyunsaturated fats. Virgin olive oil is used because it has a fine fruity flavour lacking in the lesser grade known as "pure". In addition, it is—like all olive oil—high in mono-unsaturated fats, which are thought not to increase blood cholesterol. When virgin olive oil is unavailable, or when its flavour is not essential to the success of the dish, 'pure' may be used.

About cooking times

To help planning, time is taken into account in the recipes. While recognizing that everyone cooks at a different speed and that stoves and ovens differ, approximate "working" and "total" times are provided. Working time stands for the minutes actively spent on preparation; total time includes unattended cooking time, as well as time devoted to marinating, steeping or soaking ingredients. Since the recipes emphasize fresh foods, they may take a bit longer to prepare than 'quick and easy' dishes that call for canned or packaged products, but the difference in flavour, and often in nutrition, should compensate for the little extra time involved.

Recommended Dietary Guidelines

Average Daily Intake		Maximum Daily Intake					
		Calories	Protein grams	Cholesterol milligrams	Total fat grams	Saturated fat grams	Sodium milligrams
Females 7-8		1900	47	300	80	32	2000*
	9-11	2050	51	300	77	35	2000
	12-17	2150	53	300	81	36	2000
	18-54	2150	54	300	81	36	2000
	55-74	1900	47	300	72	32	2000
Males 7-8		1980	49	300	80	33	2000
	9-11	2280	57	300	77	38	2000
	12-14	2640	66	300	99	44	2000
	15-17	2880	72	300	108	48	2000
	18-34	2900	72	300	109	48	2000
	35-64	2750	69	300	104	35	2000
	65-74	2400	60	300	91	40	2000

* (or 5g salt)

Basic Dressings with a New Twist

New Mayonnaise

Makes 35 cl (12 fl oz)
Calories 70, Protein 1g, Cholesterol 12mg, Total fat 7g,
Saturated fat 1g, Sodium 50mg

125 g/4 oz	firm tofu (bean curd), cut into small cubes and soaked in cold water for 10 minutes
12.5 cl/4 fl oz	plain low-fat yoghurt, drained in a muslin-lined colander for 10 minutes
1	egg yolk
1 tsp	dried mustard
12.5 cl/4 fl oz	safflower oil
4 tbsp	virgin olive oil
2 tbsp	white wine vinegar or cider vinegar
1/2 tsp	salt
1/2 tsp	sugar
1/8 tsp	white pepper

Remove the tofu from its soaking water and drain it on paper towels. Transfer the tofu to a food processor or a blender. Add the yoghurt, egg yolk and mustard, and process the mixture until it is very smooth, scraping down the sides at least once.

With the motor still running, pour in the oils in a thin, steady stream, stopping half way through the process to scrape the sides with a rubber spatula.

Add the vinegar, salt, sugar and pepper, and process the mayonnaise for 15 seconds more. Transfer the mayonnaise to a bowl and refrigerate it; the mayonnaise will keep for at least 10 days.

Vinaigrette

Makes about 12.5 cl (4 fl oz)
Calories 75, Protein 0g, Cholesterol 0mg, Total fat 8g,
Saturated fat 1g, Sodium 75mg

1 tsp	Dijon mustard
1/4 tsp	salt
	freshly ground black pepper
2 1/2 tbsp	red wine vinegar
2 1/2 tbsp	safflower oil
2 1/2 tbsp	virgin olive oil

In a small bowl, combine the mustard, the salt, a grinding of pepper and the vinegar. Whisking vigorously, pour in the safflower oil in a thin, steady stream; incorporate the olive oil in the same way. Continue whisking until the dressing is well combined. Covered and stored in the refrigerator, the dressing will keep for about a week.

Buttermilk Dressing

Makes about 12.5 cl (4 fl oz)
Calories 15, Protein 1g, Cholesterol 1mg, Total fat 0g,
Saturated fat 0g, Sodium 30mg

12.5 cl/4 fl oz	buttermilk
	cayenne pepper
1/4 tsp	sugar
1	shallot, finely chopped
4 tbsp	dried skimmed milk
2 tbsp	fresh lemon juice

In a small bowl, combine the buttermilk, a pinch of cayenne pepper, the sugar and the shallot. Whisk in the dried milk a tablespoon at a time, then stir in the lemon juice. To allow the dressing to thicken, cover the bowl and refrigerate it for at least 30 minutes. The dressing will keep for three days.

EDITOR'S NOTE: The inclusion of dried skimmed milk makes for a thick, creamy dressing.

Creamy Yoghurt Dressing

Makes about 12.5 cl (4 fl oz)
Calories 20, Protein 1g, Cholesterol 2mg, Total fat 1g,
Saturated fat 0g, Sodium 25mg

2 tbsp	cream sherry
2	garlic cloves, finely chopped
1 1/2 tsp	Dijon mustard
12.5 cl/4 fl oz	plain low-fat yoghurt
1 tbsp	soured cream
1/8 tsp	white pepper

Put the sherry and garlic into a small saucepan. Bring the mixture to a simmer over medium heat and cook it until nearly all the liquid has evaporated—about 3 minutes. Transfer the mixture to a bowl. Stir in the mustard, then the yoghurt, soured cream and pepper. Cover the bowl and store the dressing in the refrigerator; it will keep for two to three days.

Potato Salad with Peas and Sesame Seeds

Serves 8 as a side dish
Working time: about 25 minutes
Total time: about 1 hour and 15 minutes
Calories 140, Protein 3g, Cholesterol 0mg, Total fat 6g,
Saturated fat 1g, Sodium 70mg

750 g/1¹/₂ lb	*waxy potatoes*
500 g/1 lb	*fresh peas, shelled, or 150 g (5 oz) frozen peas, thawed*
3 tbsp	*sesame seeds*
¹/₂ tsp	*cumin seeds*
¹/₄ tsp	*cayenne pepper*
250 g/8 oz	*cucumber peeled and coarsely chopped*
5	*spring onions, trimmed and thinly sliced*
3 tbsp	*fresh lemon juice*
¹/₄ tsp	*salt*
2 tbsp	*safflower oil*
¹/₄ tsp	*turmeric*
2	*mildly hot green chilli peppers, seeded, deribbed and quartered lengthwise (caution, opposite page)*

Boil the potatoes until they are soft when pierced with the tip of a sharp knife—about 25 minutes. Remove the potatoes from the water, halve them and set them aside to cool.

Meanwhile, parboil the fresh peas until they are tender—4 to 5 minutes—or briefly blanch the frozen peas. Drain the peas and set them aside.

Heat a small, heavy frying pan over medium-high heat. When the pan is hot, add the sesame seeds, half of the cumin seeds and the cayenne pepper; toast the seeds, stirring constantly until the sesame seeds turn light gold—about 1 minute. Transfer the mixture to a large bowl and let the seeds cool.

Peel the potatoes, then cut them into slices about 8 mm (¹/₃ inch) thick, halve the slices, and put them in the bowl with the sesame seed mixture. Grind the remaining cumin with a mortar and pestle and sprinkle it over the potatoes. Add the peas, cucumber, spring onions, lemon juice and salt to the bowl. Toss the ingredients well to combine them, and set aside.

Heat the safflower oil in a heavy frying pan over medium-high heat. When the oil is hot, reduce the heat to low and stir in the turmeric; immediately add the chilli peppers and sauté them, stirring constantly, for 1 minute. Remove the chilli pepper pieces and reserve them, and pour the contents of the pan over the potato mixture. Stir the salad gently to blend it, then transfer it to a serving platter. Garnish the salad with the reserved chillies. The salad may be served at room temperature or chilled.

Chilli Peppers—a Cautionary Note

Both dried and fresh hot chilli peppers should be handled with care. Their flesh and seeds contain volatile oils that can make skin tingle and cause eyes to burn. Rubber gloves offer protection—but the cook should still be careful not to touch the face, lips or eyes when working with chilli peppers.

Soaking fresh chilli peppers in cold, salted water for an hour will remove some of their fire. If canned chillies are substituted for fresh ones, they should be rinsed in cold water in order to eliminate as much of the brine used to preserve them as possible.

Sweet and Spicy Sweetcorn Salad

Serves 12 as a side dish
Working time: about 20 minutes
Total time: about 25 minutes
Calories 105, Protein 2g, Cholesterol 0mg, Total fat 3g,
Saturated fat 0g, Sodium 60mg

825 g/1³/₄ lb	*fresh sweetcorn kernels (cut from about 5 large ears), or frozen sweetcorn kernels, thawed*
1	*sweet red pepper, seeded, deribbed and cut into thin, 2.5 cm (1 inch) long strips*
1	*sweet green pepper, seeded, deribbed and cut into thin, 2.5 cm (1 inch) long strips*
2	*small hot green chilli peppers, seeded, deribbed and finely chopped (caution, above)*
1	*small red onion, chopped*
4 tbsp	*red wine vinegar*
1 tbsp	*brown sugar*
2 tbsp	*safflower oil*
2 tsp	*chopped fresh oregano, or ¹/₂ tsp dried oregano*
¹/₄ tsp	*salt*
	freshly ground black pepper

Pour enough water into a saucepan to fill it about 2.5 cm (1 inch) deep. Set a vegetable steamer in the pan and bring the water to the boil. Put the fresh sweetcorn into the steamer, cover the pan, and steam the sweetcorn until it is just tender—about 3 minutes. (Frozen sweetcorn does not require steaming.)

In a large bowl, combine the wine vinegar, sugar, oil, oregano, salt and pepper. Add the sweetcorn, the peppers and the onion, and toss the mixture well. Serve the salad at room temperature, or refrigerate it for at least 1 hour and serve it well chilled.

Greens with Violets and Wild Strawberries

VIOLET BLOSSOMS, WHEN AVAILABLE, ADD A DELICIOUS DELICACY TO A
SIMPLE GREEN SALAD. PICK THE BLOSSOMS JUST BEFORE SERVING
TIME. DO NOT USE VIOLETS FROM A FLORIST—THEY MAY HAVE BEEN
SPRAYED WITH CHEMICALS.

Serves 4 as a first course or side dish
Working time: about 10 minutes
Total time: about 15 minutes
Calories 60, Protein 1g, Cholesterol 0mg, Total fat 5g,
Saturated fat 1g, Sodium 25mg

1 tbsp *raspberry vinegar*
1 tbsp *finely chopped shallot*
1/2 tsp *Dijon mustard*
        freshly ground black pepper
1 1/2 tbsp *unsalted chicken stock*
1 1/2 tbsp *virgin olive oil*
250 g/8 oz *mixed salad greens, washed and dried*
4 tbsp *sweet violet blossoms (optional)*
4 tbsp *wild strawberries (optional)*

Combine the vinegar, shallot, mustard and some pepper in a small bowl. Let the mixture stand for 5 minutes; whisk in the stock, then the oil. Toss the greens with the dressing. Strew the violets and the strawberries, if using, over the top; serve immediately.

EDITOR'S NOTE: The greens here include Batavian endive, chicory, watercress and red oakleaf lettuce, any similar combination of mild and bitter greens would be appropriate.

Red Cabbage Salad with Spiced Vinegar Dressing

Serves 6 as a side dish
Working time: about 15 minutes
Total time: about 1 hour and 15 minutes
Calories 100, Protein 3g, Cholesterol 0mg, Total fat 8mg,
Saturated fat 2g, Sodium 170mg

350 g/12 oz	red cabbage, finely shredded
1/2 tsp	salt
4 tbsp	red wine vinegar
1	blade of mace
1	bay leaf
8	peppercorns
1/2 tsp	mustard seeds
4	allspice
2	dried red chilli peppers
1	small sweet green pepper, seeded, deribbed and finely sliced
1	small onion, halved and finely sliced
3	sticks celery, finely sliced
30 g/1 oz	pine-nuts, lightly toasted
2 tbsp	virgin olive oil
1	garlic clove, crushed
1/4 tsp	sugar
	freshly ground black pepper

Put the shredded cabbage into a large salad bowl, sprinkle with the salt and toss lightly together. Cover the bowl and set it aside in a cool place for 1 hour.

Meanwhile, put the vinegar into a small saucepan with the mace, bay leaf, peppercorns, allspice and chilli peppers. Bring to the boil, then boil gently until the vinegar is reduced to 1 tablespoonful. Allow to cool. Add the sliced green pepper, onion, celery and toasted pine-nuts to the red cabbage.

Strain the cold vinegar into a small bowl and add the oil, garlic, sugar and freshly ground pepper to taste. Whisk lightly together. Pour this dressing over the red cabbage and toss well. Serve at once.

Wrapped Salads

Serves 6 as a first course
Working time: about 1 hour
Total time: about 1 hour and 45 min
Calories 85, Protein 2g, Cholesterol 0mg, Total fat 4g,
Saturated fat 0g, Sodium 220mg

2	fennel bulbs, green tops removed, bulbs cut into bâtonnets
250 g/8 oz	turnips, peeled and cut into bâtonnets
500 g/1 lb	courgettes, cut into bâtonnets
2	oranges, juice of 1, pared rind of both
6	large Savoy cabbage leaves
1	small red onion, finely chopped
1 1/2 tbsp	safflower oil
2 tbsp	finely chopped fresh chervil or parsley
1/2 tsp	salt
	freshly ground black pepper
6	sprigs fresh chervil or parsley for garnish

Bring 2 litres (3 1/2 pints) of water to the boil in a large pan. Place the fennel bâtonnets in a sieve; lower the sieve part way into the boiling water and blanch the bâtonnets until they are tender but still slightly crunchy—2 to 3 minutes. Refresh the fennel under cold running water, drain it well, and transfer it to a large bowl. Blanch the turnip bâtonnets the same way for 2 to 3 minutes; refresh them and transfer them to the bowl. Blanch the courgette pieces for about 1 minute; refresh them, too, and put them in the bowl.

Use the sieve to blanch the orange rind in the boiling water for 10 seconds; refresh the rind under cold running water and drain it well. Finely chop the rind and transfer it to the bowl with the bâtonnets.

Boil the cabbage leaves in the same pan of water until they are pliable but not too soft—about 15 sec-

onds. Drain the leaves; when they are cool enough to handle, use a V-shaped cut to remove the thick core from the stem end of each leaf. Set the leaves aside.

Add the onion, oil, orange juice, chopped chervil or parsley, salt and some pepper to the bowl with the bâtonnets; toss the mixture well, then refrigerate the salad for about 15 minutes.

Spread the cabbage leaves out on a work surface. Using a slotted spoon, divide the salad evenly among the leaves. Gather the edges of a leaf over its filling; gently twist the edges closed, forming a pouch. Repeat the process to enclose the other five mounds of filling.

Place the cabbage bundles in a shallow dish and pour the dressing remaining in the bowl over the top and sides of each one. Chill the salads for about 30 minutes before serving them, garnished with the chervil or parsley sprigs.

Carrot, Swede and Watercress Salad

Serves 6 as a side dish
Working (and total) time: about 40 minutes
Calories 60, Protein 1g, Cholesterol 0mg, Total fat 3g,
Saturated fat 0g, Sodium 70mg

4 tsp	virgin olive oil
3	carrots, halved lengthwise, the halves cut diagonally into 5 mm (1/4 inch) slices
325 g/11 oz	swedes, peeled and cut into bâtonnets
1	shallot, halved, the halves quartered
1/8 tsp	salt
1/4 tsp	cayenne pepper
	freshly ground black pepper
4 tbsp	cider vinegar
1	bunch of watercress, stemmed, washed and dried

Heat the oil in a large, heavy frying pan over medium

heat. When the oil is hot, add the carrots, swedes, shallot, salt, cayenne pepper and some black pepper. Cook the mixture, stirring frequently, until the vegetables are tender but still crisp—about 7 minutes. Pour the vinegar into the pan and continue cooking, stirring frequently, until almost all of the vinegar has evaporated—1 to 2 minutes. Stir in the watercress and cook it until it has just wilted—about 30 seconds. Transfer the salad to a serving plate and let it cool just slightly before serving it.

Cucumber and Citrus Salad

Serves 4 as a side dish
Working (and total) time: about 25 minutes
Calories 80, Protein 2g, Cholesterol 0mg, Total fat 1g,
Saturated fat 0g, Sodium 135mg

1	large cucumber, cut into 5 cm (2 inch) long segments
1 tsp	virgin olive oil
1 tsp	chopped fresh rosemary, or 1/4 tsp crushed dried rosemary
	freshly ground black pepper
1	pink grapefruit
2	large juicy oranges
2 tbsp	fresh lime juice
4 tbsp	fresh orange juice
4 tbsp	fresh grapefruit juice
1 tsp	red wine vinegar
1/4 tsp	salt
1	spring onion, cut into 5 cm (2 inch) long julienne

Using an apple corer, a melon baller or a small spoon, remove the core of seeds from each cucumber segment. Slice the segments into rings about 3 mm (1/8 inch) thick. Toss the rings with the oil, rosemary and a generous grinding of pepper.

Working over a bowl to catch the juice, cut away the peel, white pith and outer membrane from the grapefruit and oranges. To separate the segments from the inner membranes, slice down to the core with a sharp knife on either side of each segment; set the segments aside. Cut each grapefruit segment in half; leave the orange segments whole. Set the bowl containing the juice aside.

Arrange the cucumber slices in a large, deep plate and position the citrus segments on top. If you are preparing the salad in advance, it may be refrigerated for up to 2 hours at this point.

Combine the lime juice, orange juice, grapefruit juice, vinegar and salt with the reserved juice in the bowl. Pour this dressing over the salad; scatter the spring onion over the top just before serving.

Asparagus and Jerusalem Artichoke Salad

Serves 4 as a first course
Working (and total) time: about 20 minutes
Calories 45, Protein 2g, Cholesterol 0mg, Total fat 1g,
Saturated fat 0g, Sodium 5mg

1 *lemon, cut in half*
125 g/4 oz *Jerusalem artichokes, scrubbed well*
500 g/1 lb *asparagus, trimmed, peeled and cut*
diagonally in to 4 cm (1½ inch) lengths
1 tsp *walnut oil or virgin olive oil*
1 tbsp *cut fresh dill*

Make acidulated water by squeezing the juice of a lemon half into a small bowl of cold water. Peel and slice the Jerusalem artichokes, dropping them into the water as you work.

Pour enough water into a saucepan to fill it about 2.5 cm (1 inch) deep. Set a vegetable steamer in the pan and bring the water to the boil. Put the artichoke slices into the steamer, cover the pan tightly, and steam the slices until they are tender when pierced with a knife—about 5 minutes. Transfer the slices to a bowl and toss them with the juice of the other lemon half.

While the artichokes are steaming, cook the asparagus. Pour enough water into a large sauté pan to fill it about 2.5 cm (1 inch) deep. Bring the water to the boil, add the asparagus pieces, and cook them until they are tender—about 4 minutes. Drain the asparagus and refresh the pieces under cold water. Drain the pieces once again and toss them with the oil.

Arrange the asparagus on a large serving platter or on four small plates. Top the asparagus with the artichoke slices; sprinkle the dill all over before serving.

Julienned Carrots, Mange-Tout and Chicory

Serves 6 as a first course or side dish
Working (and total) time: about 20 minutes
Calories 60, Protein 2g, Cholesterol 0mg, Total fat 4g,
Saturated fat 0g, Sodium 70mg

1 tbsp	*very finely chopped shallot*
1	*garlic clove, lightly crushed*
1 tbsp	*herb vinegar or white wine vinegar*
1¹/₂ tbsp	*almond oil or walnut oil*
¹/₈ tsp	*salt*
	freshly ground black pepper
75 g/2¹/₂ oz	*carrots, julienned*
150 g/5 oz	*mange-tout, julienned*
250 g/8 oz	*chicory, cored and julienned*

In a large bowl, combine the shallot, garlic and vinegar. Whisk in the oil and season the dressing with the salt and some pepper. Set the dressing aside while you prepare the vegetables.

Add the carrot julienne to 1 litre (1³/₄ pints) of boiling water and cook it for 1 minute. Add the mange-tout and cook the vegetables for only 15 seconds longer. Briefly refresh the vegetables under cold running water, then drain them well. Remove the garlic from the dressing and discard it. Add the cooked vegetables and the chicory to the dressing. Toss the salad well and serve it immediately.

Six-Treasure Asian Medley

Serves 10 as a side dish
Working (and total) time: about 40 minutes
Calories 70, Protein 2g, Cholesterol 0mg, Total fat 4g,
Saturated fat 0g, Sodium 220mg

350 g/12 oz	*carrots*
125 g/4 oz	*mange-tout, strings removed*
350 g/12 oz	*small cucumbers*
4 tbsp	*sliced water chestnuts*
250 g/8 oz	*Chinese cabbage, sliced crosswise into 1 cm (¹/₂ inch) thick strips*
1	*sweet red pepper, seeded, deribbed and julienned*
Ginger-sesame dressing	
1 tsp	*Sichuan peppercorns*
1 tsp	*dry mustard*
2 tsp	*sugar*
3 tbsp	*rice vinegar*
3 tbsp	*low-sodium soy sauce or shoyu*
2 tsp	*dark sesame oil*
2 tbsp	*safflower oil*
1 tbsp	*finely chopped fresh ginger root*
3	*garlic cloves, finely chopped*

With a small paring knife or a cannelle knife, cut a shallow groove running the length of each carrot. Repeat the cut on the opposite side of each carrot, then slice the carrots diagonally into ovals about 3 mm (¹/₈ inches) thick. Put the pieces in a saucepan and pour in enough cold water to cover them by about 5 cm (2 inches). Bring the water to the boil. Reduce the heat and simmer the carrots until they are barely tender—about 2 minutes. Drain the carrots and transfer them to a large bowl.

Cut a V-shaped notch in each end of each mange-tout. Blanch them in boiling water for 30 seconds. Refresh the mange-tout under cold running water, drain them well, and add them to the bowl with the carrots.

Peel the cucumbers, leaving four narrow strips skin attached to each one. Halve the cucumbers lengthwise; scoop out the seeds with a melon baller or a teaspoon. Cut the cucumber halves into 3 mm (¹/₈ inch) thick slices. Add the cucumber slices, water chestnuts, cabbage and red pepper to the bowl containing the carrots and mange-tout.

To prepare the dressing, put the Sichuan pepper corns into a small frying pan and set it over medium-high heat. Cook the peppercorns until you see the fine wisps of smoke. Transfer the peppercorns to a mortar or a small bowl and crush them with a pestle or the heel of a heavy knife. Whisk together the mustard, sugar, vinegar, soy sauce, sesame oil, safflower oil, peppercorns, ginger and garlic. Toss the vegetable with the dressing and serve at once.

Charcoal-Grilled Summer Salad

Serves 8 as a side dish
Working time: about 1 hour
Total time: about 1 hour and 30 minutes
Calories 95, Protein 3g, Cholesterol 0mg, Total fat 5g,
Saturated fat 1g, Sodium 115mg

1	*large aubergine*
$1/2$ tsp	*salt*
2	*large courgettes*
$1/2$ tsp	*virgin olive oil*
	freshly ground black pepper
2	*sweet red peppers*
250 g/ 8 oz	*Batavian endive or rocket, stemmed, washed and dried*
4	*ripe tomatoes, halved lengthwise*
1	*small red onion, very thinly sliced*

Garlic and herb dressing

1	*whole garlic bulb, the papery top cut off to expose the cloves*
5 tsp	*virgin olive oil*
1 tbsp	*fresh lemon juice*
1 tbsp	*chopped fresh parsley*
$1/2$ tbsp	*fresh thyme, or $1/2$ tsp dried thyme*
$1/2$ tbsp	*chopped fresh oregano, or $1/2$ tsp dried oregano*
$1/8$ tsp	*salt*
	freshly ground black pepper
1 tbsp	*walnut or safflower oil*

To begin the dressing, first preheat the oven to 180°C (350°F or Mark 4). Place the garlic bulb on a piece of aluminium foil and dribble $1/2$ teaspoon of the olive oil over the exposed cloves. Fold the foil tightly around the bulb and roast the garlic until it is very soft—about 1 hour. Approximately half way through the roasting

time, light the charcoal in an outdoor barbecue. When the garlic bulb is cool enough to handle, remove the cloves from their skins and set them aside.

While the garlic is roasting, peel the aubergine and cut it lengthwise into eight slices. Sprinkle the ¹/₂ teaspoon of salt over the slices and let them stand for at least 30 minutes to neutralize their natural bitterness. Rinse the slices to rid them of the salt, and pat them dry with paper towels. Cut each of the courgettes lengthwise into four slices. Brush the aubergine and courgette slices with the ¹/₂ teaspoon of olive oil. Sprinkle the vegetables with some pepper and set them aside.

When the charcoal is hot, place the red peppers on the rack; turn them as they scorch, until their skins are blistered on all sides—10 to 15 minutes. Transfer the peppers to a bowl and cover it with plastic film; the trapped steam will loosen the skins.

Grill the aubergine and courgette slices until they are golden-brown but retain their shape—about 5 minutes per side. Remove the vegetables from the barbecue and let them cool to room temperature.

With a paring knife, peel the peppers. Seed and derib them, then quarter them lengthwise. Set the pepper pieces aside.

To finish the dressing, press the reserved garlic cloves through a sieve into a small bowl. Add the lemon juice, parsley, thyme, oregano, ¹/₈ teaspoon of salt and some pepper; stir well to combine the ingredients. Whisking vigorously, pour in the remaining olive oil in a thin, steady stream; incorporate the walnut or safflower oil the same way, and continue whisking until the dressing is thoroughly combined.

Arrange the endive or rocket on a large platter to form a bed for the other vegetables. Position the aubergine, courgettes, red peppers, tomatoes and onion in rows on the greens. Pour the dressing over the vegetables and serve.

Shiitake Mushroom Salad

Serves 4 as a first course
Working time: about 20 minutes
Total time: about 30 minutes
Calories 95, Protein 2g, Cholesterol 0mg, Total fat 5g,
Saturated fat 1g, Sodium 150mg

1¹/₂ tbsp	virgin olive oil
50 g/1¹/₂ oz	thinly sliced shallots
250 g/8 oz	fresh shiitake mushrooms or field mushrooms, stemmed and wiped clean, caps sliced
2 tsp	fresh thyme, or ¹/₂ tsp dried thyme
¹/₄ tsp	salt
2	ripe tomatoes, seeded and cut into 5 mm (¹/₄ inch) wide strips
2 tbsp	balsamic vinegar, or 1¹/₂ tbsp red wine vinegar mixed with ¹/₂ tsp honey
1 tbsp	fresh lemon juice
	freshly ground black pepper
1 tbsp	chopped fresh parsley
4	large Chinese cabbage leaves or cos lettuce leaves for garnish

Heat the olive oil in a large, heavy frying pan over medium heat. Add the shallots, mushrooms and thyme, and cook them, stirring frequently, for 7 minutes. Sprinkle with the salt, then stir in the tomatoes, vinegar, lemon juice and some pepper. Cook, stirring often, until the tomatoes are soft—about 4 minutes. Stir in the parsley and remove the pan from the heat. Let the mixture stand until it is tepid.

Place a cabbage or lettuce leaf on each of four plates; divide the salad evenly among the leaves.

Bean Sprouts in a Sesame Vinaigrette

Serves 8 as a side dish
Working time: about 10 minutes
Total time: about 25 minutes
Calories 50, Protein 2g, Cholesterol 0mg, Total fat 3g,
Saturated fat 0g, Sodium 80mg

2 tbsp *Chinese black vinegar or balsamic vinegar*
1 tbsp *low-sodium soy sauce or shoyu*
1 tbsp *safflower oil*
1 tsp *dark sesame oil*
1 1/2 tsp *sugar*
500 g/1 lb *fresh mung bean sprouts*
1 tbsp *sesame seeds*
1 *spring onion, trimmed, finely chopped*

Bring 3 litres (5 pints) of water to the boil in a large pan. While the water is heating, combine the vinegar, soy sauce, safflower oil, sesame oil and sugar in a small bowl.

Immerse the bean sprouts in the boiling water; stir them once and drain them immediately. Refresh the sprouts under cold running water, then transfer them to a bowl lined with a clean cloth; the cloth will absorb the water. Refrigerate for at least 10 minutes.

Remove the cloth, leaving the sprouts in the bowl. Pour the dressing over the sprouts and toss the salad well. Chill the salad for 5 minutes more and toss it once again. Sprinkle the sesame seeds and chopped spring onion over the top, and serve at once.

Asian-Style Cucumber Salad

Serves 6 as a side dish
Working time: about 30 minutes
Total time: about 3 hours (includes chilling)
Calories 35, Protein 0g, Cholesterol 0mg, Total fat 3mg,
Saturated fat 0g, Sodium 5mg

2 tbsp *rice vinegar*
1 *garlic clove, finely chopped*
1 tsp *finely chopped fresh ginger root*
1 tsp *mirin (sweet Japanese rice wine)*
1/4 tsp *dark sesame oil*
1 tbsp *peanut or safflower oil*
1 *large cucumber*
30 g/1 oz *carrot, julienned*
30 g/1 oz *yellow squash or courgette, julienned*
4 tbsp *radish sprouts*

Combine the vinegar, garlic, ginger, mirin, sesame oil, and peanut or safflower oil in a bowl. Set the vinaigrette aside.

With a cannelle knife or a paring knife, cut four shallow lengthwise grooves in the cucumber. Halve the cucumber lengthwise. Thinly slice the cucumber halves.

Put the cucumber, carrot, squash or courgette, and radish sprouts in the vinaigrette; stir well. Refrigerate the mixture for 2 to 3 hours before serving.

A Potpourri of Vegetables Bathed in Balsamic Vinegar

Serves 8 as a first course
Working time: about 40 minutes
Total time: about 50 minutes
Calories 80, Protein 3g, Cholesterol 0mg, Total fat 4g,
Saturated fat 1g, Sodium 135mg

2$\frac{1}{2}$ tbsp *virgin olive oil*
3 *shallots, thinly sliced*
1 *garlic clove, finely chopped*
1 *bunch beet greens with stems, washed and thinly sliced (about 125 g/4 oz)*
$\frac{1}{4}$ tsp *salt*
    freshly ground black pepper
6 tbsp *balsamic vinegar*
2 *carrots halved lengthwise and sliced diagonally into 1 cm ($\frac{1}{2}$ inch) pieces*
2 *small turnips, peeled and cut into bâtonnets*
150 g/5 oz *small broccoli florets*
250 g/8 oz *courgettes halved lengthwise and sliced diagonally into 1 cm ($\frac{1}{2}$ inch) pieces*
125 g/4 oz *small yellow squash or courgettes, halved lengthwise and sliced diagonally into 1 cm ($\frac{1}{2}$ inch) pieces*

Pour 3 litres (5 pints) of water into a large pan; add 1 teaspoon of salt and bring the water to the boil.

In the meantime, heat 1$\frac{1}{2}$ tablespoons of the oil in a large, heavy frying pan set over medium heat. Add the shallots and garlic, and cook them for 2 minutes. Stir in the beet greens and their stems, the $\frac{1}{4}$ teaspoon of salt and some pepper. Cook the mixture, stirring frequently, for 7 minutes. Pour the vinegar over the mixture, stir well, and remove the pan from the heat.

Put the carrots into the boiling water and cook them for 1 minute. Add the turnips and broccoli to the carrots in the pan, and cook them for 2 minutes. Add the courgettes and yellow squash to the pan, and cook all the vegetables together for only 30 seconds more. Immediately drain the vegetables and refresh them under cold running water when they are cool, drain them on paper towels.

Transfer the vegetables to a bowl and pour the contents of the frying pan over them. Dribble the remaining tablespoon of oil over the top, add a liberal grinding of pepper, and toss the salad well. Chill the salad for at least 10 minutes. Toss it once more before presenting it at the table

EDITOR'S NOTE: If beet greens are not available, Swiss chard leaves can be substituted.

Alfalfa Sprouts and Red Onion Salad

Serves 4 as a first course
Working (and total) time: about 15 minutes
Calories 75, Protein 1g, Cholesterol 0mg, Total fat 5g, Saturated fat 0g, Sodium 70mg

1	*large juicy orange*
1 tbsp	*fresh lemon juice*
1 tbsp	*safflower oil*
1 tsp	*virgin olive oil*
1 tsp	*fresh thyme, or $^1/_4$ tsp dried thyme*
$^1/_2$ tsp	*sugar*
$^1/_8$ tsp	*salt*
	freshly ground black pepper
1	*red onion, sliced into paper-thin rounds, the rings separated*
45 g/1$^1/_2$ oz	*alfalfa sprouts*

Working over a bowl to catch the juice, cut away the peel, white pith and outer membrane from the orange. To separate the segments from the inner membranes, slice down to the core with a sharp knife on either side of each segment and set the segments aside. Squeeze the remaining membranes over the bowl to extract any juice.

Stir the lemon juice, safflower oil, olive oil, thyme, sugar, salt and some pepper into the juice in the bowl. Whisk the dressing well.

Put the onion rings into a bowl and pour half of the dressing over them. Add a generous grinding of pepper and toss well. In the other bowl, combine the alfalfa sprouts with the remaining dressing.

Spread equal amounts of the onion rings on four plates. Mound one quarter of the sprouts in the centre of each bed of onions, then garnish each serving with the orange segments. Serve immediately.

Tomato Fans with Basil, Prosciutto and Provolone

Serves 4 as a first course or side dish
Working time: about 20 minutes
Total time: about 35 minutes
Calories 105, Protein 5g, Cholesterol 11mg, Total fat 7g,
Saturated fat 2g, Sodium 280mg

2	large ripe tomatoes, cored
$\frac{1}{4}$ tsp	sugar
$\frac{1}{8}$ tsp	salt
	freshly ground black pepper
2 tbsp	red wine vinegar
1	shallot, finely chopped
1 tbsp	virgin olive oil
2	garlic cloves, crushed
45 g/1$\frac{1}{2}$ oz	thinly sliced prosciutto, julienned
30 g/1 oz	provolone cheese, thinly sliced and julienned
2 tbsp	thinly sliced fresh basil leaves
1	round lettuce (about 125 g/4 oz), washed and dried

Halve the tomatoes from top to bottom, then, with the cut side down, thinly slice each half, and set it aside intact. Transfer the sliced halves to a plate. Gently fan out each half. Sprinkle the tomatoes with the sugar, salt and a generous grinding of black pepper, then dribble 1 tablespoon of the wine vinegar over them. Refrigerate the tomato fans for about 10 minutes.

Meanwhile, prepare the dressing. Put the finely chopped shallot and the remaining tablespoon of vinegar into a bowl. Whisk in the oil. Add the garlic, prosciutto, provolone cheese, basil and some more pepper, and stir the mixture to combine it; set it aside.

Arrange the lettuce on a serving platter and place the tomato fans on the leaves. Remove the garlic cloves from the dressing and spoon a quarter of it on each tomato fan. Serve the salad immediately.

Baby Leeks in Caper-Cream Vinaigrette

Serves 6 as a first course
Working time: about 20 minutes
Total time: about 45 minutes
Calories 190, Protein 2g, Cholesterol 3mg, Total fat 4g,
Saturated fat 1g, Sodium 200mg

12	baby leeks (about 750 g/1$\frac{1}{2}$ lb) trimmed, green tops cut to within 5 cm (2 inches) of the white part
2 tsp	fresh thyme, or $\frac{1}{2}$ tsp dried thyme
2	shallots, finely chopped
$\frac{1}{4}$ tsp	salt
	freshly ground black pepper
1 tbsp	fresh lemon juice
1 tbsp	red wine vinegar
1 tsp	capers, rinsed and chopped
1 tbsp	virgin olive oil
2 tbsp	single cream
2 tbsp	chopped sweet red pepper
1	garlic clove, very finely chopped

Wash each leek to remove the grit: without splitting the leek or detaching any leaves, gently prise apart the leaves and run cold water between them to force out the dirt. Shake the excess water from the leaves and repeat the washing process. Arrange the leeks in a pan large enough to hold them in a single layer. Pour in just enough water to cover the leeks; add the thyme, half of the shallots, $\frac{1}{8}$ teaspoon of the salt and a lavish grinding of pepper. Poach the leeks over medium-low heat for 10 minutes. Gently turn the leeks over, and continue poaching them until they are tender—about 10 minutes more. Transfer the leeks to a plate lined with a double thickness of paper towels. Refrigerate the leeks until they are cool—at least 20 minutes.

About 10 minutes before the leeks are sufficiently chilled, combine the remaining shallots in a small bowl with the lemon juice, vinegar, capers, the remaining $\frac{1}{8}$ teaspoon of salt and some more pepper. Let the vinaigrette stand for 5 minutes, then whisk in the oil, cream, red pepper and garlic.

Transfer the cooled leeks to a serving dish. Pour the vinaigrette over the leeks and serve them at once.

Curried Cabbage Coleslaw

Serves 6 as a side dish
Working time: about 20 minutes
Total time: about 1 hour and 20 minutes
Calories 60, Protein 2g, Cholesterol 4mg, Total fat 2g,
Saturated fat 1g, Sodium 145mg

15 cl/5 fl oz	*soured cream*
2 tsp	*curry powder*
2 tsp	*tomato paste*
2 tsp	*lemon juice*
¹/₂ tsp	*salt*
	freshly ground black pepper
500 g/1 lb	*white cabbage, finely shredded*
1	*red apple, quartered, cored and thinly sliced*
40 g	*raisins*
1 tbsp	*chopped fresh coriander*

Put the soured cream, curry powder, tomato paste, lemon juice, salt and some freshly ground pepper into a large bowl and stir well. Add the shredded cabbage, sliced apple and the raisins and mix well together. Cover the bowl, then set it aside in a cool place for at least 1 hour to allow the flavours to mellow.

Just before serving, spoon the salad into a serving bowl and garnish with the coriander.

Dandelion Greens
with Potato and Bacon

THE PLEASINGLY PUNGENT LEAVES OF THE DANDELION MAKE FOR A BRACING SALAD. HARVEST THE BRIGHT GREEN LEAVES IN THE SPRING; THE DARKER LEAVES THAT GROW IN THE SUMMER HAVE A BITTER TASTE.

Serves 4 as a first course
Working time: about 30 minutes
Total time: about 45 minutes
Calories 130, Protein 5g, Cholesterol 9mg, Total fat 6g,
Saturated fat 1g, Sodium 265mg

1	*large waxy potato*
1 tbsp	*safflower oil*
45 g/1¹/₂ oz	*mild back bacon, julienned*
2	*shallots, thinly sliced*
2 tbsp	*red wine vinegar*
4 tbsp	*unsalted chicken stock*
¹/₂ tsp	*sugar*
¹/₈ tsp	*salt*
	freshly ground black pepper
250 g/8 oz	*dandelion greens, washed and dried*

Boil the potato until it is barely tender—about 15 minutes. Remove the potato from the water and set it aside until it is cool enough to handle. Peel the potato and cut it into small dice.

Heat the safflower oil in a heavy frying pan over medium-high heat. Add the bacon and shallots, and sauté them until the bacon begins to brown—4 to 5 minutes. Add the diced potato and continue sautéing until the potato pieces begin to brown too—about 3 minutes more.

Stir in the vinegar and cook the mixture for 2 minutes. Add the stock, sugar, salt and some pepper; cook the mixture, stirring often, until the liquid is reduced by half—about 3 minutes.

Pour the contents of the pan over the dandelion greens and toss well; serve the salad immediately.

Moulded Leek Salads

Serves 4 as a first course
Working time: about 30 minutes
Total time: about 2 hours and 30 minutes
Calories 80, Protein 6g, Cholesterol 2mg, Total fat 1g,
Saturated fat 0g, Sodium 80mg

350 g/12 oz	*leeks, trimmed, split, washed thoroughly to remove all grit, and sliced crosswise into 5 mm (1/4 inch) thick pieces*
1/4 litre/8 fl oz	*cold unsalted chicken stock*
1 tbsp	*fresh lemon juice*
1 tbsp	*powdered gelatine*
12.5 cl/4 fl oz	*plain low-fat yoghurt*
1/2 tbsp	*Dijon mustard*
4 tbsp	*finely chopped parsley*
1 tbsp	*finely cut fresh chives*
	freshly ground black pepper
	watercress sprigs for garnish

Add the leeks to 2 litres (3 1/2 pints) of water boiling in a pan. Return the water to the boil and cook the leeks until they are tender—about 2 minutes. Drain the leeks thoroughly and allow them to cool.

In a bowl, combine half of the stock with the lemon juice. Sprinkle the gelatine on top of the liquid and allow it to soften. Meanwhile, heat the remaining stock in a small saucepan over low heat. Pour the gelatine mixture into the pan, then stir gently until the gelatine dissolves. Return the gelatine mixture to the bowl and set the bowl in a larger vessel filled with ice cubes. Whisk in the yoghurt and mustard. Chill the mixture, stirring it from time to time. When it begins to set—after about 20 minutes—fold in the leeks, parsley, chives and some pepper.

Rinse four 12.5 cl (4 fl oz) ramekins with cold water. Shake the ramekins dry, leaving a few drops of water clinging inside. Divide the leek mixture evenly among the ramekins, then chill them until the mixture is firm—about 2 hours.

To serve the moulded salads, run the tip of a knife around the inside of each ramekin. Dip the bottoms of the ramekins in hot water for about 15 seconds, then unmould the salads on to individual plates. Garnish each one with a few sprigs of watercress and serve at once.

Batavian Endive Chiffonade with Peppers

Serves 6 as a side dish
Working time: about 20 minutes
Total time: about 45 minutes
Calories 55, Protein 2g, Cholesterol 0mg, Total fat 4g,
Saturated fat 1g, Sodium 125mg

12.5 cl/4 fl oz	*unsalted veal or chicken stock*
2	*sweet black peppers, seeded and deribbed, one coarsely chopped, the other very thinly sliced*
1	*dried hot red chilli pepper, seeded and crushed (caution, page 15)*
1	*shallot, coarsely chopped*
1½ tbsp	*red wine vinegar*
¾ tsp	*sugar*
¼ tsp	*salt*
	freshly ground black pepper
1½ tbsp	*virgin olive oil*
1 tbsp	*fresh lime juice*
1	*large Batavian endive (about 750 g/1½ lb), trimmed, cut in half through core*

In a small frying pan, combine the stock, the chopped sweet pepper, chilli pepper, shallot, vinegar, sugar, salt and some pepper. Simmer over low heat, stirring frequently, until only about 3 tablespoons of liquid remain—7 to 10 minutes.

Transfer the contents of the pan to a blender. Add the oil and lime juice and purée the mixture to obtain a smooth dressing. Transfer the dressing to a large bowl; immediately add the sliced sweet pepper. Refrigerate the dressing until it is cool—about 15 minutes.

Lay an endive half on a work surface cut side down and slice it into chiffonade. Repeat the process with the other half. Toss the chiffonade with the dressing and serve the salad at once.

Gingery Cauliflower Salad

Serves 4 as a first course or side dish
Working time: about 20 minutes
Total time: about 45 minutes
Calories 60, Protein 1g, Cholesterol 0mg, Total fat 0g,
Saturated fat 0g, Sodium 150mg

1	cauliflower, trimmed and cut into florets
2.5 cm/1 inch	piece fresh ginger root, peeled and julienned
1	carrot, julienned
2 tbsp	white vinegar
1/2 tsp	sugar
1/4 tsp	salt
1/8 tsp	cayenne pepper
1 tbsp	safflower oil
1/4 tsp	dark sesame oil
1	spring onion, trimmed, green part julienned and soaked in iced water, white part sliced diagonally into thin ovals.

Mound the cauliflower florets on a heatproof plate to resemble a whole head of cauliflower. Scatter the ginger and carrot julienne over the cauliflower.

Combine the vinegar, sugar, salt and cayenne pepper in a small bowl. Whisk in the safflower oil and pour the dressing over the cauliflower.

Pour enough water into a large pan to fill it about 2.5 cm (1 inch) deep. Stand two or three small heatproof bowls in the water and set the plate with the cauliflower on top of the bowls. Cover the pan, bring the water to the boil and steam the cauliflower until it can be easily pierced with a knife—15 to 20 minutes.

Remove the lid and let the steam dissipate. Lift the plate out of the pan and let the cauliflower stand until it cools to room temperature. Dribble the sesame oil over the cauliflower and scatter the green and white spring onion on top. Serve the salad at room temperature or chilled.

Apricots and Water Chestnuts in Wild Rice

Serves 8 as a side dish
Working time: about 30 minutes
Total time: about 1 hour
Calories 130, Protein 4g, Cholesterol 0mg, Total fat 0g,
Saturated fat 0g, Sodium 75mg

160 g/5¹/₂ oz wild rice
125 g/4 oz dried apricots, cut into 1 cm (¹/₂ inch)
         pieces
175 g/6 oz fresh water chestnuts, peeled and
         quartered, or 250 g (8 oz) canned whole
         peeled water chestnuts, drained rinsed
         and quartered
2 tbsp chopped parsley
Spicy lemon dressing
2 tbsp fresh lemon juice
1 tbsp red wine vinegar
¹/₈ tsp ground ginger
¹/₈ tsp cinnamon
         ground cloves
¹/₄ tsp salt
         freshly ground black pepper

Bring 1.5 litres (2¹/₂ pints) of water to the boil in a sauce-pan. Stir in the wild rice, reduce the heat, and simmer the rice, uncovered, until it is tender but still chewy—approximately 45 minutes.

While the rice cooks, prepare the apricots and dressing: put the apricots into a small bowl and pour in enough hot water to cover them by about 2.5 cm (1 inch). Soak the apricots for 20 minutes to soften them. Drain the apricots, reserving 4 tablespoons of their soaking liquid, and set them aside.

Pour the reserved apricot-soaking liquid into a small bowl. Add the lemon juice, vinegar, ginger, cinnamon, a pinch of cloves, the salt and some pepper; whisk the mixture vigorously until it is thoroughly combined.

When the rice finishes cooking, drain and rinse it, and transfer it to a serving bowl. Pour the dressing over the rice, then add the apricots, water chestnuts and the parsley; toss the ingredients well and serve the salad at room temperature.

Endive Salad with Orange and Rosemary

Serves 6 as a first course or side dish
Working (and total) time: about 25 minutes
Calories 70, Protein 2g, Cholesterol 0mg, Total fat 4g,
Saturated fat 1g, Sodium 150mg

1 garlic clove, cut in half
1 head of curly endive, washed and dried
3 small heads of chicory, washed, dried and
    sliced crosswise into 1 cm (1/2 inch) wide
    strips
1 navel orange
1 small red onion, thinly sliced
1 tbsp chopped fresh rosemary, or 1 tsp dried
    rosemary, crumbled
1/8 tsp salt
2 tbsp sherry vinegar or red wine vinegar

1 tbsp grainy mustard
1 1/2 tbsp virgin olive oil

Rub the inside of a salad bowl with the cut surfaces of the garlic clove. Put the endive and chicory into the bowl. Working over a bowl to catch the juice, cut away the peel, white pith and outer membrane from the flesh of the orange. To separate the segments from the membranes, slice down to the core with a sharp knife on either side of each segment and set the segments aside. Cut each segment in thirds and add them to the bowl along with the onion and rosemary.

In a small bowl, whisk together the salt, reserved orange juice, vinegar and mustard. Whisking constantly, pour in the oil in a thin, steady stream to create an emulsified dressing. Pour the dressing over the contents of the salad bowl; toss the salad thoroughly and serve it at once.

the sweet potatoes into the steamer, cover the pan tightly, and steam the sweet potatoes until they are just tender—about 10 minutes. Transfer the sweet potatoes to a large bowl and set them aside.

Steam the beans until they are cooked but still crisp—about 4 minutes. Refresh the beans under cold running water to preserve their colour, then add them to the bowl with the sweet potatoes.

While the beans are cooking, prepare the dressing: combine the vinegar and soy sauce in a small bowl. Whisk in the oils, then the chilli pepper, ginger, garlic and some black pepper.

Pour all but 2 tablespoons of the dressing over the sweet potatoes and beans; add the spring onions and toss well. Chill the vegetables for at least 1 hour.

To serve the salad, toss the cabbage with the remaining 2 tablespoons of dressing and transfer it to a serving plate. Mound the chilled vegetables on top and scatter the peanuts over all.

Sweet Potato Salad with Peanuts

Serves 8 as a side dish
Working time: about 30 minutes
Total time: about 1 hour and 30 minutes
Calories 150, Protein 4g, Cholesterol 0mg, Total fat 4g,
Saturated fat 0g, Sodium 140mg

750 g/1¹/₂ lb	*sweet potatoes, peeled, halved length-wise and cut into 5 mm (¹/₄ inch) thick slices*
250 g/8 oz	*french beans, trimmed and cut in half*
3	*spring onions, trimmed and thinly sliced*
750 g/1¹/₂ lb	*Chinese cabbage, sliced into chiffonade*
2 tbsp	*coarsely chopped dry-roasted unsalted peanuts*

Ginger dressing

4 tbsp	*rice vinegar*
1 tbsp	*low-sodium soy sauce or shoyu*
1 tbsp	*safflower oil*
1 tsp	*dark sesame oil*
1	*hot green chilli pepper, seeded, deribbed and finely chopped*
1 tbsp	*finely chopped fresh ginger root*
1	*garlic clove, finely chopped*
	freshly ground black pepper

To cook the sweet potatoes, pour enough water into a saucepan to fill it about 2.5 cm (1 inch) deep. Set a steamer in the pan and bring the water to the boil. Put

Artichoke Bottoms in Mango and Red Onion Dressing

Serves 6 as a first course or side dish
Working time: about 40 minutes
Total time: about 1 hour
Calories 70, Protein 1g, Cholesterol 0mg, Total fat 2g,
Saturated fat 0g, Sodium 75mg

8	*large globe artichokes*
1	*lemon, cut in half*
7	*ripe mango, peeled, the flesh cut into small cubes*
1¹/₂ tbsp	*fresh lemon or lime juice*
1 tbsp	*red wine vinegar*
1 tbsp	*virgin olive oil*
¹/₈ tsp	*salt*
	freshly ground black pepper
60 g/2 oz	*red onion, chopped*

To prepare the artichoke bottoms, first break or cut the stem off one of the artichokes. Snap off and discard the outer leaves, starting at the base and continuing until you reach the pale yellow leaves at the core. Cut the top two thirds off the artichoke. Trim away any dark green leaf bases that remain on the artichoke bottom. Rub the artichoke all over with a lemon half to keep it from discolouring. Repeat these steps to prepare the remaining artichoke bottoms.

Heat 12.5 cl (4 fl oz) of water in a large, non-reactive sauté pan over low heat. Put the artichoke bottoms into the water, tightly cover the pan, and steam them for 7 minutes. Turn them over, cover the pan again, and continue steaming until tender when pierced with a knife—about 7 minutes more. Transfer the artichokes to a plate and refrigerate them.

While the artichokes are cooking, prepare the dressing. Put the mango, lemon or lime juice, vinegar, oil, salt and some pepper into a food processor or blender. Purée the mixture, scraping down the sides at least once during the process. Transfer the dressing to a large bowl and stir in the onion.

When the artichokes are cool, scrape out the chokes with a spoon. Cut each artichoke into 12 wedges and stir them into the mango dressing. Chill the salad for at least 10 minutes before serving it.

Chicory and Watercress Salad

Serves 6 as a first course or side dish
Working (and total) time: about 30 minutes
Calories 70, Protein 2g, Cholesterol 0mg, Total fat 5g,
Saturated fat 1g, Sodium 140mg

  2 *heads of chicory*
  1 *bunch watercress, stemmed, washed
     and dried*
 12 *mushrooms, stems trimmed, caps wiped
     clean and thinly sliced*
 18 *cherry tomatoes, halved*
     Dill-mustard vinaigrette
1 tbsp *herb-flavoured mustard or Dijon mustard*
2 tbsp *finely cut fresh dill, or 1¹/₂ tbsp dried dill*
  3 *spring onions, trimmed, green parts*
     *reserved for another use, white parts
     finely chopped*
1¹/₂ tbsp *fresh lemon juice*
 ¹/₄ tsp *salt*
     freshly ground black pepper
1 tbsp *safflower oil*
1 tbsp *virgin olive oil*

To make the vinaigrette, combine the mustard, dill, spring onions, lemon juice, salt and some pepper in a small bowl. Whisking vigorously, pour in the safflower oil in a thin, steady stream; incorporate the olive oil the same way. Set the vinaigrette aside

Separate the chicory leaves from their cores. Arrange the chicory leaves, watercress, mushrooms and tomatoes on individual plates. Spoon the vinaigrette over the salad and serve immediately.

Broccoli and Chinese Cabbage Salad with Black Vinegar Dressing

Serves 8 as a side dish
Working (and total) time: about 25 minutes
Calories 40, Protein 2g, Cholesterol 0mg Total fat 2g, Saturated fat 0g, Sodium 120mg

2	*broccoli stalks, florets separated from stems, stems peeled and sliced diagonally*
1	*daikon radish (mooli)*
300 g/10 oz	*Chinese cabbage, sliced into 1 cm (1/2 inch) pieces*
1 tbsp	*safflower oil*
1/4 tsp	*dark sesame oil*

Black vinegar dressing

1/2 litre/16 fl oz	*unsalted chicken stock*
4	*thin slices peeled fresh ginger root*
1 tsp	*Sichuan peppercorns*
1/4 tsp	*sugar*
2 tbsp	*Chinese black vinegar or balsamic vinegar*
1 tbsp	*low-sodium soy sauce or shoyu*

To make the dressing, first pour the stock into a small saucepan set over medium-high heat. Add the ginger, peppercorns and sugar, and bring the liquid to the boil. Cook the mixture until it is reduced to about 12.5 cl (4 fl oz)—10 to 12 minutes.

While the stock is reducing, cook the broccoli. Pour enough water into a saucepan to fill it about 2.5 cm (1 inch) deep. Set a vegetable steamer in the water and add the broccoli florets and stems. Cover the pan tightly, bring the water to the boil, and steam the broccoli until it is barely tender—about 2 minutes. Transfer the broccoli to a bowl and refrigerate it until serving time.

Remove the reduced stock from the heat and let it cool. Stir in the vinegar and soy sauce, then strain the dressing into a small serving bowl.

Slice the daikon radish into 5 cm (2 inch) lengths. Stand one of the pieces on end; using a small, sharp knife, cut down the sides to remove the peel, giving the radish five sides. Repeat the process to fashion the remaining radish pieces. Thinly slice the pieces; keep them in iced water until serving time.

Drain the radish slices, pat them dry with paper towels, and transfer them to a large bowl along with the broccoli and cabbage. Combine the safflower oil and sesame oil; dribble the oils over the vegetables, toss well and serve. Pass the dressing separately.

39

Chayote Fans in a Coriander Vinaigrette

Serves 4 as a first course
Working time: about 25 minutes
Total time: about 45 minutes
Calories 60, Protein 1g, Cholesterol 0mg, Total fat 4g,
Saturated fat 0g, Sodium 80mg

1	*large chayote about (350 g/12 oz)*
	quartered and seeded
1 tbsp	*red wine vinegar*
¹/₂ tsp	*Dijon mustard*
1 tbsp	*safflower oil*
1 tbsp	*chopped fresh coriander*
¹/₂ tsp	*sugar*
¹/₈ tsp	*salt*
	freshly ground black pepper
1	*large dried mild chilli pepper, cut in half*
	lengthwise and seeded
4	*fresh coriander sprigs for garnish*

Cut a chayote quarter lengthwise into thin slices, leaving the slices attached at the tapered end to form a fan. Repeat the process with the other quarters.

Pour enough water into a saucepan to fill it about 2.5 cm (1 inch) deep. Set a vegetable steamer in the pan and bring the water to the boil. Set the chayote fans in the steamer, cover the pan, and steam the vegetable until it is barely tender—4 to 5 minutes. Transfer the chayote to a shallow bowl.

Cut the lemon in half. Slice one half into four rounds and reserve the rounds for garnish. Squeeze enough juice from the other half to measure 1 tablespoon and pour it into a small mixing bowl. Add the vinegar and mustard, and whisk in the oil. Season the vinaigrette with the coriander, sugar, salt and some pepper. Pour the vinaigrette over the chayote fans and chill them.

Meanwhile, place the chilli pepper in a small bowl, pour ¹/₄ litre (8 fl oz) of boiling water over it, and let it soak for 20 minutes. Remove the chilli pepper from its soaking liquid; do not discard the liquid. Put the pepper pieces in a blender along with 4 tablespoons of the soaking liquid. Drain the vinaigrette from the chilled chayote and add it to the pepper pieces and liquid. Purée the dressing and strain it through a fine sieve.

Spoon the dressing on to four individual salad plates. Transfer the chayote fans to the plates and place a sprig of coriander on each fan. Garnish each salad with a lemon round.

40

Sweet Potato Salad with Curried Yoghurt Dressing

Serves 6 as a side dish
Working time: about 30 minutes
Total time: about 2 hours (includes chilling)
Calories 120, Protein 3g, Cholesterol 2mg, Total fat 1g,
Saturated fat 0g, Sodium 60mg

500 g/1 lb *sweet potatoes*
4 *sticks celery, thinly sliced*
3 *spring onions, trimmed and thinly sliced*
12.5 cl/4 fl oz *yoghurt dressing (recipe, page 13) mixed with 1¹/₂ tsp curry powder*
1 tbsp *each finely cut chives and chopped parsley, or 2 tbsp chopped parsley*

Put the sweet potatoes in a deep saucepan and pour in enough water to cover them. Bring the water to the boil and cook the sweet potatoes over medium heat until they are tender—25 to 30 minutes. Drain the sweet potatoes; when they are cool enough to handle, peel them and cut them into small dice. Put the sweet potatoes in a bowl with the celery and spring onions.

Add the dressing to the vegetables and mix gently. Chill the salad for at least 1 hour. Just before serving, sprinkle the fresh herbs over the top.

EDITOR'S NOTE: this salad makes a delicious accompaniment to grilled chicken or pork.

Courgette and Apple in Rice Vinegar

Serves 8 as a side dish
Working (and total) time: about 20 minutes
Calories 30, Protein 1g, Cholesterol 0mg, Total fat 1g, Saturated fat 0g, Sodium 35mg

250 g/8 oz *courgettes, julienned*
1 *green apple, peeled, cored, julienned*
1 *red apple, quartered, cored, thinly sliced*
1 tsp *chopped fresh tarragon, or ¹/₂ tsp dried*
tarragon
1 tsp *safflower oil*
2 tbsp *rice vinegar*
¹/₈ tsp *salt*
freshly ground black pepper

In a large bowl, combine the courgettes, apples and
tarragon. Add the oil and toss the mixture to coat the
salad. Stir in the vinegar, salt and some pepper; toss
the salad and serve it at once.

Kohlrabi Salad

Serves 6 as a side dish
Working (and total) time: about 40 minutes
Calories 45, Protein 3g, Cholesterol 3mg, Total fat 2g,
Saturated fat 0g, Sodium 45mg

500 g/1 lb	*kohlrabies or turnips, peeled and shredded*
4 tbsp	*diced pimiento*
1 tbsp	*fresh lemon juice*
12.5 cl/4 fl oz	*yoghurt dressing (recipe, page 13)*

Pour 2 litres (3¹/₂ pints) of cold water into a saucepan. Add the kohlrabi or turnip shreds, bring the water to the boil, then blanch for 2 minutes. Drain them in a colander, refresh them under cold running water, and drain them again. Rid the vegetables of excess moisture by pressing down on them with the back of a large spoon. (Or wrap them in muslin and wring out.)

Transfer the kohlrabi or turnip shreds to a bowl and stir in the pimiento and lemon juice. Pour the dressing over the top, toss the salad well, and serve it at once.

Sautéed Greens with Red Potatoes and Apple

Serves 8 as a side dish
Working time: about 25 minutes
Total time: about 1 hour and 25 minutes
Calories 105, Protein 2g, Cholesterol 2mg, Total fat 3g,
Saturated fat 1g, Sodium 150mg

1	*large tart apple*
1 tbsp	*fresh lemon juice*
500 g/1 lb	*red potatoes, scrubbed and cut into 2 cm (³/₄ inch) cubes*
¹/₂ tsp	*salt*
1 tbsp	*red wine vinegar*
1¹/₂ tbsp	*virgin olive oil*
1	*shallot finely chopped*
250 g/8 oz	*spinach, spring greens, Swiss chard leaves or young kale, stemmed, washed, torn into 5 cm (2 inch) pieces and dried*
12.5 cl/4 fl oz	*milk*
	freshly ground black pepper

Peel, quarter and core the apple, and cut it into 2 cm (³/₄ inch) pieces. In a small bowl, toss the apple with the lemon juice; set the bowl aside.

Pour ¹/₂ litre (16 fl oz) of water into a saucepan. Add the potatoes and salt, and bring the water to the boil. Reduce the heat and simmer the potatoes for 10 minutes. Add the apple to the saucepan and continue cooking the mixture, stirring often so that it does not burn, until only 2 tablespoons of liquid remain—about 10 minutes more.

Combine the wine vinegar and ¹/₂ tablespoon of the olive oil in a small bowl. Pour this mixture over the hot potatoes and apple, and set them aside.

Heat the remaining oil in a large, heavy frying pan over medium heat. Cook the shallot in the oil for 1 minute. Add the greens and cook them, stirring frequently, until they are wilted—about 3 minutes. Pour in the milk and continue cooking the mixture until all the liquid has evaporated—7 to 10 minutes.

Combine the potato mixture, the greens and a generous grinding of pepper in a large bowl. Toss the salad well and refrigerate it for at least 45 minutes. Toss it once more before serving.

French Beans with Creamy Horseradish Dressing

Serves 8 as a first course
Working time: about 40 minutes
Total time: about 1 hour and 15 minutes
Calories 55, Protein 3g, Cholesterol 1mg, Total fat 1g,
Saturated fat 0g, Sodium 115mg

2	*sweet red peppers*
8	*globe artichokes*
1	*lemon, halved*
250 g/8 oz	*French beans, trimmed*
250 g/8 oz	*okra, trimmed*

Horseradish dressing

12.5 cl/4 fl oz	*plain low-fat yoghurt*
4 tbsp	*grated horseradish*
1 tsp	*celery seeds*
1 tsp	*fresh lemon juice*
1/4 tsp	*salt*
1 tbsp	*chopped fresh thyme, or 1 tsp dried thyme*
3 tbsp	*chopped parsley*
1/8 tsp	*cayenne pepper*
	freshly ground black pepper

Roast the peppers about 5 cm (2 inches) below a preheated grill, turning them until the skins have blistered on all sides. Transfer the peppers to a bowl and cover it with plastic film; the trapped steam will loosen the skins. When the peppers are cool enough to handle, peel, seed and derib them, and cut them into 5 mm (1/4 inch) cubes.

To prepare each artichoke bottom, first break or cut off the stem. Snap off and discard the outer leaves, starting at the base and continuing until you reach the pale yellow leaves at the core. Cut the top two thirds off the artichoke. Trim away any dark green leaf bases that remain on the artichoke bottom. Rub the artichoke all over with one of the lemon halves.

Fill a large, non-reactive saucepan with water and bring it to the boil. Squeeze the juice of both lemon halves into the water, then add the lemon halves themselves. Add the artichoke bottoms to the boiling water and cook them until they can be easily pierced with the tip of a sharp knife—about 15 minutes. Drain the artichoke bottoms and refresh them under cold running water. Using a teaspoon, scrape the furry choke from each artichoke bottom. Rinse and drain the bottoms, and cut each one into eight pieces.

Pour enough water into a large saucepan to fill it about 2.5 cm (I inch) deep. Set a vegetable steamer in the pan and bring the water to the boil. Put the French beans into the steamer, cover the pan tightly, and steam the beans until they are tender—about 6 minutes. Lift out the steamer; refresh the beans under cold running water, then drain them well, and set them aside.

Return the steamer to the pan and bring the water to the boil. Set the okra in the steamer, cover the pan tightly, and steam the okra until it is barely tender—about 3 minutes. Remove the okra from the pan and refresh it under cold running water. Cut each okra in half lengthwise and set it aside

To prepare the dressing, whisk together the yoghurt horseradish, celery seeds, lemon juice, salt, thyme, parsley, cayenne pepper and some black pepper in a large bowl. Add the beans, artichoke bottoms, okra and all but 2 tablespoons of the red peppers to the dressing. Toss well and serve the salad with the reserved red pepper cubes sprinkled on top.

Carrot and Orange Salad with Dill

Serves 4 as a side dish
Working time: about 10 minutes
Total time: about 25 minutes
Calories 90, Protein 2g, Cholesterol 0mg, Total fat 0g,
Saturated fat 0g, Sodium 50mg

1	*large juicy orange*
600 g/1 1/4 lb	*carrots, finely grated*
1 tbsp	*red wine vinegar*
12.5 cl	*fresh orange juice*
1/2 tsp	*grated orange rind*
2 tbsp	*fresh dill*

Working over a bowl to catch the juice, cut away the peel, white pith and outer membrane from the orange. To separate the segments from the inner membranes, slice down to the core with a sharp knife on either side of each segment and set the segments aside.

Combine the carrots, vinegar, orange juice and rind in the bowl. Add the orange segments and 1 tablespoon of the dill; gently toss the ingredients. Refrigerate the salad for at least 15 minutes. Shortly before serving, garnish the top with the remaining dill.

Red, White and Green Salad

Serves 6 as a first course or side dish
Working time: about 20 minutes
Total time: about 1 hour
Calories 60, Protein 2g, Cholesterol 0mg, Total fat 4g,
Saturated fat 0g, Sodium 75mg

250 g/8 oz	beetroot, rinsed
3 tbsp	raspberry vinegar or red wine vinegar
2 tsp	Dijon mustard
2 tsp	grainy mustard
1/4 tsp	honey
	freshly ground black pepper
1 1/2 tbsp	virgin olive oil
1	head of radicchio, halved, cored, washed, dried and cut into chiffonade (opposite)
1	large head of chicory, cored, cut in half crosswise, the halves julienned
125 g/4 oz	lamb's lettuce (corn salad or mâche), washed and dried, or one small lettuce, washed, dried and torn into pieces

Put the beetroot into a saucepan, pour in enough water to cover, and bring the water to the boil. Cook the beetroot until it is tender—about 30 minutes. Drain

46

the beetroot and let it cool before peeling and finely dicing it. Put the diced beetroot in a small bowl, and toss it with 1 tablespoon of the vinegar.

To make the dressing, combine the mustards, the honey, the remaining vinegar and a liberal grinding of pepper in a bowl. Whisk in the oil.

In another bowl, toss the radicchio and chicory with two thirds of the dressing. Separately toss the lamb's lettuce with the remaining dressing.

To assemble the salad, mound the radicchio-chicory mixture in the centre of a platter and surround it with the lettuce. Scatter the diced beetroot on top.

Cutting Chiffonade

1 Rolling the leaves. Pluck the leaves from a head of spinach, cabbage or lettuce (here, radicchio). Gently wash and dry the leaves. Stack three to four leaves and roll them into a bundle.

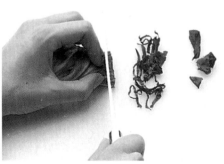

2 Cutting the roll. Holding the bundle with your fingers curled under for safety, square the end by cutting off the rounded tips of the leaves. Slice across the roll at approximately 3 mm (¹/₈ inch) intervals to produce the thin strips called chiffonade.

Spinach and Sesame Salad

Serves 6 as a side dish
Working (and total) time: about 30 minutes
Calories 60, Protein 4g, Cholesterol 0mg, Total fat 5g,
Saturated fat 0g, Sodium 255mg

12.5 cl/4 fl oz	*unsalted chicken stock*
1 tbsp	*sesame seeds*
1 tbsp	*tahini (sesame paste)*
1 tsp	*dark sesame oil*
1¹/₂ tbsp	*low-sodium soy sauce or shoyu*
1 tbsp	*fresh lemon juice*
1 tsp	*finely chopped fresh ginger root*
500 g/1 lb	*spinach, washed, stemmed and dried*
125 g/4 oz	*mushrooms, wiped clean and thinly sliced*
1	*large ripe tomato, sliced into thin wedges*
¹/₈ tsp	*salt*
	freshly ground black pepper

Boil the stock in a small saucepan until only 2 tablespoons remain—about 7 minutes.

While the stock is reducing, toast the sesame seeds in a small, heavy frying pan over medium-low heat until they are golden—about 3 minutes. Set the pan aside.

To prepare the dressing, mix the tahini and sesame oil in a small bowl. Whisk in the reduced stock, the soy sauce, lemon juice and ginger.

Put the spinach and mushrooms into a large bowl. Sprinkle the tomato wedges with the salt and pepper and add them to the bowl. Pour the dressing over the vegetables, grind in some more pepper, and toss well. Scatter the sesame seeds over the salad and serve.

Kale Pear and Goat Cheese Salad

Serves 8 as a first course
Working (and total) time: about 40 minutes
Calories 90, Protein 4g, Cholesterol 5mg, Total fat 4g,
Saturated fat 1g, Sodium 200mg

1¹/₂ tbsp	virgin olive oil
500 g/1 lb	onions, thinly sliced
¹/₄ tsp	salt
500 g/1 lb	kale, stemmed and washed, large leaves torn in half
12.5 cl/4 fl oz	cider vinegar
60 g/2 oz	thinly sliced pancetta (Italian bacon) or prosciutto, cut into thin strips
1	pear, quartered, cored and thinly sliced lengthwise
	freshly ground black pepper
60 g/2 oz	fresh goat cheese, broken into small pieces

Heat 1 tablespoon of the olive oil in a large, heavy frying pan over medium heat. Add the onions and ¹/₈ teaspoon of the salt; cook the onions, scraping the browned bits from the bottom of the pan vigorously and often, until the onions are caramelized—25 to 30 minutes.

Meanwhile, cook the kale in 3 litres (5 pints) of boiling water for 7 minutes. Drain the kale and refresh it under cold running water. When the kale has cooled thoroughly, mould it into a ball and squeeze out as much liquid as possible.

When the onions are caramelized, stir the vinegar into the pan, scraping up any remaining pan deposits. Continue cooking the mixture until most of the liquid has evaporated—about 5 minutes.

Heat the remaining oil in a smaller frying pan over medium heat. Cook the pancetta or prosciutto in the oil for 1 minute, add it to the onion mixture, then stir in the kale, the sliced pear, the remaining salt and a generous grinding of black pepper. Stir in half of the goat cheese.

Divide the mixture among eight plates; dot the tops of the portions with the remaining cheese and serve the salad immediately.

Chilled Celeriac, Carrot and Yellow Pepper Salad

Serves 6 as a side dish
Working time: about 15 minutes
Total time: about 1 hour and 15 minutes
Calories 45, Protein 1g, Cholesterol 0mg, Total fat 2g, Saturated fat 0g, Sodium 90mg

250 g/8 oz	*celeriac, scrubbed*
2 tbsp	*red wine vinegar*
1	*carrot, peeled and julienned*
1	*sweet yellow pepper, seeded, deribbed and cut into thin strips*
1 tbsp	*safflower oil*
1/4 tsp	*sugar*
1/8 tsp	*salt*

Peel and julienne the celeriac. To prevent discoloration, transfer the pieces to a bowl and sprinkle them with the vinegar; toss the pieces well to coat them. Add the carrot, yellow pepper, oil, sugar and salt, and toss thoroughly to combine all the ingredients. Cover and refrigerate for at least 1 hour before serving.

49

Lettuce Leaves in a Garlicky Vinaigrette

Serves 6 as a first course or side dish
Working time: about 10 minutes
Total time: about 25 minutes
Calories 110, Protein 3g, Cholesterol 0mg, Total fat 5g,
Saturated fat 1g, Sodium 150mg

1	*whole garlic bulb, the cloves separated and peeled*
1 tbsp	*balsamic vinegar, or 3/4 tbsp red wine vinegar mixed with 1/4 tsp honey*
1 tbsp	*virgin olive oil*
1 tbsp	*safflower oil*
1/8 tsp	*salt*
	freshly ground black pepper
2	*large round lettuces, leaves washed and dried*
12	*thin French bread slices, toasted*

Put the garlic cloves into a small saucepan and pour in enough water to cover them. Bring the liquid to the boil, then reduce the heat, and simmer the garlic until it is quite tender—about 15 minutes. Increase the heat and boil the liquid until only about 2 tablespoons remain—2 to 3 minutes.

Pour the contents of the saucepan into a sieve set over a small bowl. With a wooden spoon, mash the garlic through the sieve into the bowl. Whisk the vinegar into the garlic mixture, then incorporate the olive oil, safflower oil, salt and some pepper.

Toss the lettuce leaves with the dressing; garnish the salad with the toast and serve at once.

Potato Salad with Roasted Red Pepper Sauce

Serves 8 as a side dish
Working (and total) time: about 40 minutes
Calories 110, Protein 2g, Cholesterol 0mg, Total fat 4g,
Saturated fat 0g, Sodium 70mg

750 g/1 1/2 lb	*round red potatoes or other waxy potatoes, scrubbed*
2	*sweet red peppers*
2	*garlic cloves, peeled and crushed*
1 tsp	*chopped fresh rosemary, or 1/2 tsp dried rosemary, crumbled*
1/4 tsp	*salt*
	cayenne pepper
2 tbsp	*red wine vinegar*
2 tbsp	*virgin olive oil*
175 g/6 oz	*rocket, washed and dried, or 2 bunches watercress, stemmed, washed and dried*

Put the potatoes into a large saucepan and cover them with cold water. Bring the water to the boil and cook the potatoes until they are tender when pierced with the tip of a sharp knife—about 25 minutes. Drain the potatoes and set them aside to cool.

While the potatoes are boiling, roast the peppers about 5 cm (2 inches) below a preheated grill, turning them often, until they are blistered on all sides. Put the peppers into a bowl and cover the bowl with plastic film; the trapped steam will loosen their skins. Peel the peppers, then seed and derib them. Put the pepper into a food processor or a blender along with the garlic, rosemary, salt and a pinch of cayenne pepper. Purée the mixture to obtain a smooth sauce. With the motor still running, pour in the vinegar, then continue blending the sauce until it is well combined.

Cut the potatoes in half and then into wedges. Arrange the wedges on a bed of rocket leaves or watercress. Pour some of the sauce over the potatoes and serve the rest alongside.

51

Grilled Aubergine with Mint

Serves 6 as a side dish
Working time: about 25 minutes
Total time: about 50 minutes
Calories 70, Protein 2g, Cholesterol 0mg, Total fat 3g, Saturated fat 0g, Sodium 190mg

500 g/1 lb	*aubergine, cut into 2.5 cm (1 inch) cubes*
1/2 tsp	*salt*
2 tbsp	*balsamic vinegar, or 1/2 tbsp red wine vinegar mixed with 1/2 tsp honey*
125 g/4 oz	*mushrooms, wiped clean and quartered*
1/2	*lemon, juice only*
2	*ripe tomatoes, skinned, seeded and cut into strips*
1 tbsp	*sliced fresh mint leaves*

Peppery orange dressing

1	*orange, juice only*
1	*lemon, juice only*
1	*garlic clove, finely chopped*
1/8 tsp	*hot red pepper flakes*
1/4 tsp	*salt*
1 tbsp	*virgin olive oil*

Toss the aubergine cubes with the salt and let them stand for 30 minutes to make them less bitter. Rinse the cubes and pat them dry with paper towels.

Preheat the grill. Put the aubergine cubes into a fire-proof dish and grill them, stirring often, until they are browned—about 5 minutes. Transfer them to a bowl and mix in the vinegar. Set the bowl aside.

Put the mushrooms into a non-reactive saucepan with the lemon juice; pour in enough water to cover the mushrooms and simmer them over medium heat for about 5 minutes. Set the saucepan aside.

To make the dressing, combine the orange juice, lemon juice, garlic, red pepper flakes and salt in a small saucepan. Bring the mixture to the boil and cook it until the liquid is reduced by half—about 5 minutes. Remove the pan from the heat and whisk in the oil.

Arrange the aubergine cubes and tomato strips on a large plate. Drain the mushrooms and scatter them over the top. Pour the dressing over the vegetables, then sprinkle the fresh mint on top. Serve the salad at room temperature.

Broad Bean Salad

Serves 6 as a first course or side dish
Working time: about 40 minutes
Total time: about 50 minutes
Calories 125, Protein 6g, Cholesterol 3mg, Total fat 3g,
Saturated fat 1g, Sodium 95mg

2 tsp	*virgin olive oil*
1	*large onion, thinly sliced*
1	*large garlic clove. finely chopped*
125 kg/2¹/₂ lb	*fresh broad beans, shelled and peeled, or 150 g (5 oz) frozen broad beans*
30 g/1 oz	*paper-thin slices of prosciutto, julienned*
750 g/1¹/₂ lb	*ripe tomatoes, skinned, seeded and coarsely chopped, or 400 g (14 oz) canned tomatoes, chopped, with juice*
¹/₄ litre/8 fl oz	*unsalted chicken stock, or 12.5 cl (4 fl oz) unsalted chicken stock if canned tomatoes are used*
1 tbsp	*chopped fresh oregano, or 1 tsp dried oregano*
¹/₂ tsp	*cracked black peppercorns*
2 tbsp	*balsamic vinegar, or 1¹/₂ tbsp red wine vinegar mixed with ¹/₂ tsp honey*

Heat the oil in a heavy frying pan over medium heat. Add the onion slices and cook them until they are translucent—4 to 5 minutes. Stir in the garlic and cook the mixture for 1 minute more. Add the beans, prosciutto, tomatoes, stock, oregano and peppercorns. Bring the liquid to a simmer and cook the mixture until the beans are just tender—8 to 10 minutes. Transfer to a bowl and refrigerate. When the salad is cool, pour in the vinegar, toss well and serve at once.

French Bean Salad with Gruyère and Grainy Mustard

Serves 6 as a first course or side dish
Working time: about 15 minutes
Total time: about 30 minutes
Calories 70, Protein 3g, Cholesterol 8mg, Total fat 5g,
Saturated fat 2g, Sodium 120mg

350 g/12 oz	*French beans, trimmed, halved diagonally*
1	*shallot, finely chopped*
1¹/₂ tbsp	*grainy mustard, or 1 tbsp Dijon mustard*
3 tbsp	*red wine vinegar*
1 tbsp	*virgin olive oil*
¹/₈ tsp	*salt*
	freshly ground black pepper
45 g/1¹/₂ oz	*Gruyère cheese, julienned*

Pour enough water into a large saucepan to fill it about 2.5 cm (1 inch) deep. Set a vegetable steamer in the pan and bring the water to the boil. Put the beans into the steamer, cover the pan, and cook the beans until they are just tender—7 to 8 minutes. Refresh the beans under cold running water, when they are cool, drain them on paper towels.

Mix the shallot, mustard, vinegar, oil, salt and some pepper in a large bowl. Add the cheese and beans, and toss them well. Refrigerate the salad for 10 minutes. Toss it once again just before serving.

Summer Vegetables in Tomato Aspic

Serves 16 as a side dish
Working time: about 30 minutes
Total time: about 4 hours and 30 minutes (includes chilling)
Calories 50, Protein 3g, Cholesterol 0mg, Total fat 1g,
Saturated fat 0g, Sodium 50mg

250 g/8 oz	*fresh sweetcorn kernels (cut from 2 small ears), or frozen sweetcorn kernels, thawed*
800 g/28 oz	*canned tomatoes, puréed in a food processor or blender*
1	*cucumber, seeded and chopped*
¹/₂	*sweet red pepper, seeded, deribbed and chopped*
¹/₂	*sweet green pepper, seeded deribbed and chopped*
1	*small onion, finely chopped*
1 tbsp	*red wine vinegar*
6	*drops Tabasco sauce*
¹/₄ tsp	*celery seeds*
¹/₄ tsp	*salt*
	freshly ground black pepper
2 tbsp	*powdered gelatine*
35 cl/12 fl oz	*cold unsalted chicken or vegetable stock*
1	*large round lettuce, washed and dried*

If you are using fresh sweetcorn, pour enough water into a sauce pan to fill it about 2.5 cm (1 inch) deep. Set a vegetable steamer in the pan and bring the water to the boil. Put the fresh sweetcorn into the steamer; frozen sweetcorn does not require steam-

ing. Tightly cover the pan and steam the sweetcorn for 3 minutes.

In a large bowl, combine the puréed tomatoes, the cucumber, red and green pepper, onion, sweetcorn, vinegar, oil, Tabasco sauce, celery seeds, salt and some pepper. Set the bowl aside.

Stir the gelatine into 12.5 cl (4 fl oz) of the stock and set the mixture aside for 1 to 2 minutes. Bring the remaining stock to the boil, then remove it from the heat; add the gelatine-stock mixture and stir until the gelatine is dissolved.

Add the gelatine and stock to the vegetables and stir well to distribute the gelatine evenly. Pour the mixture into a 2 litre (3 pint) mould and chill it until it is firm—at least 4 hours.

Shortly before serving the salad, run the tip of a knife round the inside of the mould to loosen the sides. Briefly dip the bottom of the mould in hot water. Invert a plate on top of the mould, then turn both over together; if necessary, tap the bottom of the mould to free the salad. Lift away the mould and garnish the salad with the lettuce. Serve the salad immediately.

Broccoli Salad with Oven-Roasted Mushrooms

Serves 8 as a first course or side dish
Working (and total) time: about 1 hour and 15 minutes
Calories 105, Protein 6g, Cholesterol 0mg, Total fat 4g,
Saturated fat 0g, Sodium 150mg

1 kg/2 lb	*mushrooms, wiped clean, stems trimmed*
4	*large shallots, thinly sliced lengthwise*
6 tbsp	*fresh lemon juice*
2¹/₂ tbsp	*fresh thyme, or 2 tsp dried thyme*
¹/₄ tsp	*salt*
	freshly ground black pepper
1 tbsp	*safflower oil*
125 kg	*broccoli, stemmed and cut into florets*
1	*red or green-leaf lettuce, washed and dried*

Mustard dressing

2 tbsp	*grainy mustard*
3 tbsp	*balsamic vinegar, or 2 tbsp red wine vinegar mixed with 1 tsp honey*
1 tbsp	*chopped parsley*
2 tsp	*chopped fresh oregano, or ¹/₂ tsp dried oregano*
	freshly ground black pepper
1 tbsp	*safflower oil*

Preheat the oven to 230°C (450°F or Mark 8). Put the mushrooms in a large baking dish. Add the shallots, lemon juice, thyme, salt, some pepper and the tablespoon of oil; toss the mixture to coat the mushrooms. Spread the mushrooms in a single layer, then roast them until they are tender and most of the liquid has evaporated—20 to 25 minutes. Remove the mushrooms from the oven and keep the dish warm.

While the mushrooms are cooking, make the dressing. Combine the mustard, vinegar, parsley, oregano and some pepper in a small bowl. Whisking vigorously, pour in the tablespoon of oil in a thin, steady stream. Continue whisking until the dressing is well combined; set the dressing aside.

Pour enough water into a saucepan to fill it about 2.5 cm (1 inch) deep. Set a vegetable steamer in the pan and bring the water to the boil. Put the broccoli florets into the steamer, cover the pan, and steam the broccoli until it is tender but still crisp—about 4 minutes. Add the broccoli to the dish with the mushrooms. Pour the dressing over the vegetables and toss the salad well. Arrange the salad on a bed of the lettuce leaves; it may be served warm or chilled.

Mango and Grape Salad with Cardamom Yoghurt Dressing

THIS RECIPE CALLS FOR DRIED SKIMMED MILK, WHICH SERVES TO
THICKEN THE DRESSING

Serves 8 as a first course or side dish
Working (and total) time: about 50 minutes

Calories 110, Protein 4g, Cholesterol 2mg, Total fat 1g,
Saturated fat 0g, Sodium 30mg

4 *cardamom pods, or ¼ tsp ground*
cardamom
1 tsp *finely grated fresh ginger root*
½ litre/8 fl oz *plain low-fat yoghurt*
2 tbsp *fresh orange juice*
1 tbsp *honey*
2 tbsp *dried skimmed milk*
1 *cos lettuce, washed and dried*

3 *firm mangoes, peeled and cut into 1 cm*
(½ inch) cubes
350 g/12 oz *seedless red or green grapes, or a mixture*
of both, halved
1 tbsp *coarsely chopped unsalted pistachio nuts*

Remove the cardamom seeds from their pods and
grind them with a mortar and pestle. Place the ground
spice in a bowl and add the ginger, yoghurt, orange
juice, honey and dried milk. Whisk the ingredients together. Let the dressing stand at room temperature
for at least 20 minutes to thicken it and to allow the
different flavours to meld.

To assemble the salad, arrange the lettuce leaves
on individual plates and spoon the mango and grapes
on to the lettuce. Pour the dressing over each salad
and sprinkle the chopped pistachios on top. Serve at
once.

Midsummer Melon Salad with Almond Oil

Serves 6 as a first course or side dish
Working time: about 30 minutes
Total time: about 1 hour and 30 minutes (includes chilling)
Calories 120, Protein 2g, Cholesterol 0mg, Total fat 3g,
Saturated fat 0g, Sodium 70mg

1 *large Charentais melon, seeded, the flesh
  cut into 4 cm (1½ inch) long pieces*
½ *Gallia or Ogen melon, seeded, the flesh
  cut in to 4 cm (1½ inch) long pieces*
½ *honeydew melon, seeded, the flesh cut
  into 4 cm (1½ inch) long pieces*
1 tbsp *coarsely chopped fresh ginger root*
⅛ tsp *salt*
  freshly ground black pepper
4 tbsp *rice vinegar*
1 tbsp *almond or walnut oil*

Combine all the melon pieces in a bowl.

Using a mortar and pestle, crush the chopped fresh ginger with the salt and a generous grinding of pepper. Pour in the rice vinegar and continue crushing to extract as much juice from the ginger as possible. Working over the bowl containing the melon, strain the ginger-vinegar mixture through several layers of muslin; twist the corners of the muslin in your hands and squeeze hard so as to extract the last few drops of liquid from the ginger.

Dribble the almond or walnut oil over the melon pieces and gently toss them to distribute the dressing. Serve the salad well chilled.

Savoury Fruit Salad in Red Wine Jelly

Serves 12 as a side dish
Working time: about 30 minutes
Total time: about 4 hours and 30 minutes (includes chilling)
Calories 110, Protein 2g, Cholesterol 0mg, Total fat 0g,
Saturated fat 0g, Sodium 5mg

³/₄ litre/1¹/₄ pints	*red wine*
4 tbsp	*sugar*
1 tbsp	*fresh lemon or lime juice*
10	*black peppercorns*
1	*cinnamon stick, broken into pieces*
1¹/₂ tbsp	*powdered gelatine, softened in 2 tbsp cold water*
2	*apricots or 1 peach, stoned and cut into 1 cm (¹/₂ inch) pieces*
1	*firm yellow apple, quartered, cored and cut into 1 cm (¹/₂ inch) pieces*
2	*red plums, stoned and cut into 1 cm (¹/₂ inch) pieces*
160 g/5¹/₂ oz	*seedless green grapes, halved*
160 g/5¹/₂ oz	*sweet cherries, halved and stoned*
300 g/10 oz	*strawberries, stemmed and quartered, any very large quarters cut in half*

Fresh Fruit Salad with Cranberry Dressing

Serves 8 as a side dish
Working time: about 15 minutes
Total time: about 25 minutes
Calories 105, Protein 1g, Cholesterol 0mg, Total fat 4g,
Saturated fat 0g, Sodium 40mg

45 g/1¹/₂ oz	*fresh cranberries, or frozen cranberries, thawed*
4 tbsp	*white vinegar*
1 tbsp	*honey*
¹/₂ tbsp	*finely chopped shallot*
¹/₈ tsp	*salt*
2 tbsp	*safflower oil*
4	*tart red apples, cored and cut into cubes*
325 g/11 oz	*seedless green grapes, halved*
1	*lemon, juice only*
1	*large round lettuce, washed and dried*

Put the cranberries, vinegar and honey in a small saucepan and bring the mixture to the boil. Reduce the heat to medium low and simmer the mixture until the cranberries are quite soft and the juice has thickened—about 5 minutes. Purée the mixture in a food processor or blender, then strain it through a fine sieve. Set the cranberry purée aside and allow it to cool to room temperature.

¹/₄ tsp	*ground cinnamon*
¹/₈ tsp	*ground cloves*
	freshly ground black pepper

To prepare the wine jelly, first pour the wine into a large, non-reactive saucepan; add the sugar, lemon or lime juice, peppercorns and cinnamon stick. Bring the liquid to the boil, then lower the heat to medium and simmer the mixture until it is reduced by half—about 15 minutes. Strain the liquid through a fine sieve into a large bowl. Add the gelatine to the liquid and stir until the gelatine dissolves. Put the bowl into the refrigerator.

When the wine jelly has cooled and become syrupy, stir in the fruit, ground cinnamon, cloves and a generous grinding of pepper. Pour the salad into a 2 litre (3¹/₂ pint) mould and chill it until it is firm—about 4 hours.

To unmould the salad, run the tip of a knife around the inside of the mould to loosen the sides. Briefly dip the bottom of the mould into hot water. Invert a plate on top of the mould, then turn both over together; if necessary, rap the bottom of the mould to free the salad. Lift away the mould and serve the salad at once.

EDITOR'S NOTE: This salad deliciously complements roast lamb, pork or beef, or grilled chicken breasts

Whisk the shallot, salt and oil into the cooled purée. Toss the apples and grapes with the lemon juice. Arrange the lettuce leaves on eight individual plates and spoon the fruit on to the leaves. Ladle the purée evenly over the salad.

Brown Rice and Mango Salad

Serves 8 as a side dish

Working time: about 20 minutes

Total time: about 1 hour and 30 minutes

Calories 140, Protein 2g, Cholesterol 0mg, Total fat 4g,
Saturated fat 0g, Sodium 70mg

185 g/6¹/₂ oz *brown rice*
4 tbsp *red wine vinegar*
¹/₄ tsp *salt*
2 tbsp *safflower oil*
1 *sweet green pepper, seeded and deribbed*
1 *small shallot, finely chopped*
¹/₈ tsp *ground cardamom*
mace

cayenne pepper
1 *ripe mango, peeled and diced*

Bring 1.5 litres (2¹/₂ pints) of water to the boil in a large saucepan. Stir in the rice, reduce the heat and simmer the rice, uncovered, until it is tender—about 35 minutes. Drain the rice and put it in a serving bowl. Stir in the vinegar and salt, and allow the mixture to cool to room temperature—about 30 minutes.

When the rice is cool, stir in the oil, pepper, shallot, cardamom and a pinch each of mace and cayenne pepper. Add the mango pieces and stir them in gently so that they retain their shape. Cover the salad; to allow the flavours to meld, let the salad stand, unrefrigerated, for about 30 minutes before serving it.

Buckwheat Groats with Wild Mushrooms and Peas

Serves 6 as a side dish
Working (and total) time: about 45 minutes
Calories 110, Protein 4g, Cholesterol 0mg, Total fat 3g,
Saturated fat 0g, Sodium 90mg

7 g/¹/₄ oz	*dried wild mushrooms*
750 g/1¹/₂ lb	*fresh peas, shelled, or 250 g (8 oz) frozen peas, thawed*
200 g/7 oz	*buckwheat groats (kasha)*
250 g/7 oz	*fresh mushrooms, wiped clean, stems trimmed*
4 tbsp	*fresh lemon juice*
1 tbsp	*balsamic vinegar, ³/₄ tbsp red wine vinegar mixed with ¹/₄ tsp honey*
1	*small shallot, finely chopped*
¹/₄ tsp	*salt*
	freshly ground black pepper
1 tbsp	*safflower oil*

Soak the dried mushrooms in ¹/₄ litre (8 fl oz) of very hot water for 20 minutes, then drain them, reserving their soaking liquid. Chop the mushrooms and set them aside. If you are using fresh peas, boil them until they are tender—5 to 7 minutes (Frozen peas do not re-quire boiling but can be blanched briefly.) Drain the peas and set them aside.

While the mushrooms are soaking, add the buckwheat groats to ¹/₂ litre (16 fl oz) of boiling water and cook, stirring frequently, until tender—about 5 minutes. Drain them, rinse well, and drain again. Transfer them to a large bowl.

Slice the fresh mushrooms and put them into a small bowl with the lemon juice; the juice will prevent them from discolouring. Toss the mushrooms well and set the bowl aside.

To prepare the dressing, strain the reserved soaking liquid through a muslin-lined sieve into a small saucepan. Cook the liquid over medium-high heat until only about 2 tablespoons remain—approximately 5 minutes. Pour the liquid into a small bowl; add the lemon juice from the bowl containing the fresh mushrooms, then add the vinegar, shallot, salt and some pepper. Stir the ingredients together. Whisking vigorously, pour in the oil in a thin, steady stream. Continue whisking until the dressing is well combined. Set the dressing aside.

Add the peas, the dried and fresh mushrooms, and the dressing to the buckwheat groats. Combine the ingredients well and serve the salad at once.

Millet Tabbouleh

TABBOULEH, A MIDDLE EASTERN SALAD, IS TRADITIONALLY MADE WITH
BURGHUL. HERE MILLET PROVIDES A NEW TOUCH.

Serves 6 as a side dish
Working time: about 15 minutes
Total time: about 1 hour (includes chilling)
Calories 160, Protein 4g, Cholesterol 0mg, Total fat 4g,
Saturated fat 0g, Sodium 80mg

175 g/6 oz	*millet*
¹/₈ tsp	*salt*
	freshly ground black pepper
6 tbsp	*raisins*
100 g/3¹/₂ oz	*stemmed parsley sprigs*
1	*shallot, finely chopped*
2 tbsp	*finely chopped fresh coriander*
2 tbsp	*fresh lemon juice*
2 tsp	*honey*
2 tsp	*Dijon mustard*
1 tbsp	*safflower oil*
1	*large round lettuce, washed and dried*

Pour ¹/₂ litre (16 fl oz) of water into a saucepan and
bring it to a simmer over medium heat. Stir in the millet, salt and a generous grinding of pepper. Cover the
pan and cook the millet until the water level drops just
below the surface of the millet—10 to 15 minutes.
Stir in the raisins and reduce the heat to low; continue
cooking the millet, covered, until all the water has been
absorbed—about 7 minutes more.

Transfer the contents of the pan to a large bowl.
Immediately stir in the parsley sprigs; the hot millet
will cook them slightly. Loosely cover the bowl with
plastic film and allow the millet to cool.

Meanwhile, combine the shallot, coriander, lemon
juice, honey and mustard in a small bowl. Whisk in the
oil. When the millet has cooled to room temperature,
pour the dressing over it and toss the salad well. Serve
chilled with the lettuce.

Polenta Salad with Ham

Serves 6 as a first course or side dish
Working time: about 40 minutes
Total time: about 50 minutes
Calories 140, Protein 4g, Cholesterol 5mg, Total fat 4g,
Saturated fat 1g, Sodium 220mg

4 tsp	*salt*
1 tsp	*dried oregano, or 1 tbsp chopped fresh oregano*
125 g/4 oz	*cornmeal*
1 tbsp	*virgin olive oil*
3	*spring onions, trimmed and sliced, white parts kept separate from green*
500 g/1 lb	*ripe tomatoes, skinned, seeded, chopped*
4 tbsp	*red wine vinegar.*
	freshly ground black pepper
60 g/2 oz	*cooked ham, diced*

Bring 55 cl (18 fl oz) of water to the boil in a large
saucepan with ¹/₈ teaspoon of the salt and half of the
oregano. Sprinkle in the cornmeal, stirring continuously
with a wooden spoon. Reduce the heat to medium
and cook the polenta, stirring constantly, until all the
liquid has been absorbed and the polenta quite stiff—
10 to 15 minutes. Spoon the polenta on to a large,
lightly oiled plate and spread it out to a uniform thickness of about 1 cm (¹/₂ inch). Refrigerate the polenta
uncovered while you prepare the dressing. Preheat
the oven to 180°C (350°F or Mark 4).

Heat the oil in a heavy frying pan over medium.

Add the white spring onion parts and the remaining
oregano, and cook them for 1 minute. Stir in tomatoes, vinegar, the remaining salt and some pepper.
Cook the mixture, stirring occasionally, for 15 minutes.
Transfer the contents of the pan to a blender or food
processor, and purée the mixture until smooth dressing results. Pour the dressing into a bowl and chill it
while you finish the salad.

Cut the polenta into strips about 1 cm (¹/₂ inch) wide
and 4 cm (1¹/₂ inches) long. Transfer the strips to a
lightly oiled baking sheet and bake them for 10 minutes to dry them out, turning them occasionally with a
metal spatula. Immediately transfer the strips to the
bowl with the dressing. Add the green spring onion
parts, the ham and a generous grinding of pepper. Toss
the salad well and serve it without delay.

Saffron Rice Salad
with Peppers and Chick-Peas

Serves 12 as a side dish

Working time: about 30 minutes

Total time: about 2 hours and 45 minutes

Calories 180, Protein 5g, Cholesterol 0mg, Total fat 7g,
Saturated fat 1g, Sodium 145mg

135 g/4¹/₂ oz	dried chick-peas, picked over
¹/₄ tsp	salt
275 g/9 oz	long-grain rice
60 cl/1 pint	unsalted chicken stock or water
¹/₂ tsp	saffron threads, soaked for 10 minutes in very hot water
1	strip lemon rind
500 g/1 lb	fresh peas, shelled, or 150 g (5 oz) frozen peas, thawed
30 g/1 oz	whole unskinned almonds
1	sweet red pepper, seeded, deribbed and cut into thin slices
1	sweet green pepper, seeded, deribbed and cut into thin slices
2	ripe tomatoes, seeded and chopped
6	oil-cured black olives, thinly sliced
6 tbsp	vinaigrette

Rinse the chick-peas under cold running water. Put the chick-peas in a large, heavy pan and pour in enough cold water to cover them by about 5 cm (2 inches). Discard any chick-peas that float to the surface. Cover the pan, leaving the lid ajar, and bring the water to the boil; cook for 2 minutes. Turn off the heat, cover the pan, and soak the peas for at least 1 hour. (Alter- natively, soak the chick-peas overnight in cold water.)

When the chick-peas finish soaking, drain them well in a colander. Return them to the pan and pour in enough water to cover them by about 5 cm (2 inches). Bring the liquid to a simmer; cook the chick-peas over medium-low heat until they are soft—about 45 min- utes. Stir in the salt and continue cooking the chick- peas until they are quite tender—10 to 15 minutes more. (If the chick-peas appear to be drying out at any point, pour in more water.)

About 20 minutes before the chick-peas finish cook- ing, start the rice: bring the stock or water to the boil in a saucepan, then add the rice, the saffron and its soaking liquid, and the lemon rind. Stir the rice to dis- tribute the saffron and return the liquid to the boil. Cover the pan and cook the rice over medium-low heat until it is tender and has absorbed all the liquid—about 20 minutes. Discard the lemon rind.

While the rice is cooking, boil the fresh peas until they are tender—5 to 7—minutes. (Frozen peas do not require boiling but can be blanched briefly.) Drain the peas and set them aside. Heat the almonds in a small, heavy frying pan over medium heat, stirring fre- quently until they are lightly roasted—about 5 minutes

Drain the chick-peas well and transfer them to a large bowl. Add the rice, peas, toasted almonds, red and green peppers, tomatoes and olives. Pour the prepared vinaigrette over the salad and toss the ingredants well Transfer the salad to a serving dish. Serve at room tem- perature or barely chilled.